The Business of Beauty

Your Guide to Happiness and Success in the Salon Industry

Carrie Herzner

DEDICATION

This book is dedicated to my clients, colleagues and mentors, past and present. Thank you for the joy you've brought to my life.

CONTENTS

THE BUSINESS OF BEAUTY

ACKNOWLEDGMENTS

First and foremost, I'd like to thank my husband Brandon for his love and encouragement. This book could not have happened without his support. Thanks to my mom and mother-in-law, for the hours they've spent helping me with baby Leo. Writing a book with a newborn has its challenges, and without their help this project would have taken many years to complete. I'd also like to thank my mom for securing my first salon job for me. I'm so thankful she had a manicure that fateful day. To my sons, Liam and Logan, for putting up with all the time I spend writing. (I'm sorry for all the frozen pizza you've had to endure, though I'm quite sure you see that as a positive to my work and writing schedule.) To Rob Henschel, Andrea Jagello, and Angela Packer for your contributions to this project; Trish McKinley, for always believing in me; Sheila Cohen, for insisting I write this book; my super-fun clientele for sharing their hair experiences with me; and Stephanie Turner, for your amazing editing and proofreading skills.

1
SO YOU WANT TO BE A HAIRSTYLIST?
That's Great—Hairdressers Are Amazing!

"Hairdressers are a wonderful breed. You work one-on-one with another human being and the object is to make them feel so much better and to look at themselves with a twinkle in their eye." ~ Vidal Sassoon

Have you ever thought about becoming a hairstylist—wondered what it's really like, if you'll succeed, if you'll be happy and if working in the salon industry will be right for you? Are you currently a hairdresser and have found yourself wanting more from your career, but you're not sure what you need to do to be happy and successful? Or are you presently in cosmetology school, and are wondering what the future holds? If so, this book's for you.

Entering the world of hair design means so much more than "doing hair." In fact, hair is secondary to what you're really doing—which is connecting and communicating with people from all walks of life, assisting them in their pursuit of matching their inner beauty with their outward appearance. You're sharing your gift—your eye for design, your ability to work with your hands and your words—with every person you come into contact with at the salon. Mastering how to communicate and connect with people is just as important as mastering a perfect haircut.

This is a book about what it's really like to work in the salon industry, with advice from current stylists and salon owners, plus testimonials from clients—giving insight into what they look for in a stylist, their best and worst experiences, and how they feel when they enter the salon. It is equally a book for you, the stylist (or soon to be one)—giving you the tools needed to make sure you are taking care of the most important person behind the chair—you. It is only by taking care of *your* needs—finding the right salon to work in, setting goals and educating yourself—that you will able to properly take care of and connect with the very important people sitting in your chair... your clients.

The salon—a place where people come together, conversations flow, art and real life merge seamlessly. It can be an amazing and rewarding work environment. But you must be prepared and educated when you make the craft your calling.

John Steinbeck, one of the most prolific writers of our time, eloquently sums up the role of the hairstylist in any community:

"It is my considered opinion that the hairdresser is the most influential person in any community. When the public goes to a hairdresser, something happens to them. They feel safe, they relax. The hairdresser knows what their skin is like under the makeup, they know their age, they don't have to keep up any kind of pretense. People tell a hairdresser things they wouldn't dare confess to a priest and they are open about matters they'd try to conceal from a doctor. When people place their secret lives in the hairdresser's hands, the hairdresser gains an authority few other people attain. I have heard hairdressers quoted with complete conviction on art, literature, politics, economics, child care and morals. I tell you that a clever, thoughtful, ambitious hairdresser wields a power beyond comprehension of most people."

You are a gift. Your talent is needed and appreciated, and always will be.

So let's make the best of it, shall we?

2

THE SALON ENVIRONMENT

The Pretty and the Not-So-Pretty

"Far and away the best prize that life offers is the chance to work hard at work worth doing."
~ Theodore Roosevelt

Which of the following statements do you feel truly describe what it's like to work in the salon industry?

Hair salons are awesome and working at a salon can be a pleasure.

Hair salons are exhausting and working at a salon can be a drag.

Both statements are correct. The question is, which experience do you want to have?

I began working in the salon industry when I was fifteen years old. My mother was getting a manicure at a salon by our house, and on that fateful day the salon's front desk receptionist failed to show up for work. My mother overheard a conversation and discovered this was a common issue with the receptionist. My mother knew I'd be perfect for the job. She spoke up, telling the manager she had a daughter looking for a job, and not only was I 'very responsible for my age' (thanks, Mom) but that I also had a 'thing' for hair. And just like that, I was employed at the front desk of a salon that had sixteen hairstylists, three nail technicians, multiple phone lines, and five tanning beds. In some way or another, I was responsible for all of the above.

I fell in love.

I loved my job.

I loved going to work each day.

I knew exactly what I wanted to be when I grew up.

A salon is a little community away from the outside world. It's often an oasis and a retreat for both the clients who support the business and the stylists employed there. Where else can you go to work each day, have fun, and help others look and feel great? Salons touch all of our senses—from the smell and taste of the coffee constantly brewing, to the sounds of the hairdryers, the music, and conversation—not to mention the spontaneous eruption of laughter that seems to always be occurring. Then there's the art—art you mold and shape and create through sight and touch—the hair transforming right before your eyes. The salon is fascinating and inspiring. And people love how they feel when they're getting their hair done. Simply put, hair salons are a lot of fun.

I live in a neighborhood with twenty-seven hair salons. That's right. Twenty-seven. And, they're all busy. My neighborhood has barber shops, upscale spas and everything in between. You can't throw a glance and not see a hair salon.

This is good news for you. People will always need their hair done. Until the day we might evolve into a bald species, a good hairdresser will always be sought after. Salons come in all shapes and sizes, giving you the luxury of choice when it comes to deciding where to make your career happen.

For all the good times and great hair to be had, there's also the not-so-pretty side to working in a salon. This you should know, if you don't already. Throw a bunch of creative extroverts into a room and watch drama unfold. This side of the salon is often what we see in movies and on reality TV. More often than not, problems within the salon begin in the back of the salon, in the breakroom. The salon breakroom is intended to give stylists a place to sit, prop their feet up, shove a little food down their throats, and grab a few minutes of rest whenever we have a break in our day. (By the way, if you want to eat lunch in a civilized manner, mark time out on your book. If you don't make the time, be prepared to eat while standing in between clients, often with only five minutes at a time to spare. I feel the need to tell you this right away.) However, besides operating as it should—as a break from the floor—it also can become the salon's hub of negativity. It's where stylists vent. If you're wise, and you want to be happy and successful, you'll stay away from the breakroom gossip trap. I can't stress how important this piece of advice can be. Know that working in a salon is a lot of fun, but is also a lot of work. It is high-energy, sometimes high-stress, and both physically and mentally draining. Some stylists tend to retreat to the breakroom to complain, bringing everyone else in the room down. They complain about their clients, their boss, their schedule, their life... As a hairdresser, you're going to have several moments of anxiety, and you have to learn to take control and work through them as a professional, not an amateur. We all know people who complain, and then we know the people who do something instead of complaining. *Be a doer, not a complainer.* You are in charge of your own destiny.

If you have an issue, take control of your situation and talk to the right person—not all your coworkers, and not in the breakroom. Find your employer, your manager, your mentor, or simply listen to your gut and find a solution to your issue. And if you find that you're unsatisfied (i.e. complaining) quite often, you're most likely working in a salon that's not a good fit for you. Don't try to rally the masses by starting a coup, or have a melt-down midway through your day, and distance yourself from co-workers who do. That drama only plays well in the movies and on TV. Teamwork is essential in a salon. We all have to work together; some days are harder than others, yet few things are as rewarding, personally as well as professionally, as a busy, productive day in the salon. With the right clientele, in the right salon, with the right teammates, and a professional mindset, you can end each day satisfied.

The salon can be one of the most inspiring environments to work in. Take a look around. Look at all the art taking place, all the bonding between people. Salons are amazing, they truly are, and being a hairstylist is a unique and challenging career. Success does not come easy. You will have to work, and you will have to work hard. I've seen too many talented hairdressers walk away before ever reaching their potential. The purpose of this book is to help you avoid that fate. The salon should be a pleasant place to go to work each day, giving you the freedom to focus on what you're really there to do—which is to make money doing great hair on your amazing clientele.

Remember, being a hairdresser requires you master the delicate balance between art and psychology. Stylists must possess both visual and technical skills, but more importantly you must perfect the art of taking care of your personal needs and your clients' personal needs. Being a hairdresser requires mental and physical stamina, patience, a sharp eye and an even sharper pair of shears. It *is* hard work, and the road will not always be glossy and shiny. But if you stay positive and focused on your clients, your goals and your career, the salon environment is ridiculously fun, rewarding, lucrative, and satisfying.

3
LIFE AFTER COSMETOLOGY SCHOOL
The Apprenticeship

"The delicate balance of mentoring someone is not creating them in your own image, but giving them the opportunity to create themselves." ~ Steven Spielberg

People often ask me which cosmetology school they should attend. My answer? The nicest one you can afford. I believe you should reach for the top and invest in your career from the beginning. However, if you live in a small town, or money is tight, or you can only go part-time, go to the school that works best for you. Because guess what? It's what you do after graduating that matters the most. If you have desire and passion, no matter where you go to school you will succeed. The salon industry is not a business where a secure job is handed to you post graduation to maintain.

You have to know what you want and then you have to go and get it.

So, let's say you've graduated—invested between 1500-2100 hours of your life and an enormous amount of money. Now what?

Many graduates become an apprentice as the next step towards becoming an employed hair stylist. It's often the best step to take, and the training can be quite valuable. Apprenticing, when done properly, is time spent taking your skills to the next level and learning hands-on what life's really like behind the chair.

It can also be a huge waste of time if you're apprenticing at the wrong salon under the wrong people.

So, how do you pick the right salon? It can be very intimidating. (I've said this before, and I'll say it again. You can't throw a glance and not see a hair salon. There is a perfect salon for you.) Do not be intimidated. Make a list of salons you think you might like to work at, and then visit all of them.

You'll want to begin looking into salons while you're in cosmetology school. Your instructors can be valuable resources during your search. Some cosmetology schools are brand and technique specific—Aveda, Redken, Vidal Sassoon and Paul Mitchell come to mind. They often will assist you in finding a salon that is part of their hair care family. In some ways that makes sense—you know their color line, cutting techniques, products... but don't let that limit your options. I went to a school that only used Redken products, but worked for an Aveda distributor while I was in cosmetology school. When I graduated, I went to work at a salon that was not exclusively limited to either brand, and I loved the salon and the different color and product choices available to me. The key is to take your time, look at all the options, and ask good questions while you're talking to the owners and/or managers of the salons you're comparing.

When visiting prospective salons, take a look around, and be your most observant. Most likely you will have some time alone in the lobby before talking with the owner or manager. Absorb what's happening. Do the people seem friendly? Do the stylists and clients look happy? Are you inspired by what you see? Are members of the salon team making eye contact with you as they walk by, acknowledging you with a smile or at least a kind glance? This speaks volumes. You may be working with these people. Is the waiting area full? If yes, is that because the salon is busy or is it because the stylists are running behind? The former is good; the latter, a warning sign. Often stylists are booked improperly, and clients pay the price by waiting and waiting. Take a look at the faces of the people waiting. Expressions should tell you if they are waiting happily or if they are annoyed. Look at the stylists. Are they frazzled? Observe the front desk. Is it run smoothly, or does it look like traffic at rush hour? Does the front desk staff seem competent and happy? The front desk can be your best friend or worst nightmare once you begin booking your own clientele. Observe all that's happening around you.

Take a notebook and record your observations. Have a list of questions that are important to you ready for when the interview process begins.

Here is a brief list of qualities to look for, questions to ask, and things to take into consideration:

- Does the salon market itself and continuously attract new clients?

- Does the salon have a strong web presence?

- On average, do hairstylists tend to stay there?

- What do they pay their apprentices?

- Is there a contract involved?

- How long does the apprenticeship last?

- What type of training does being an apprentice include?

Now let's break these questions down a bit.

You should seek a salon that does some sort of marketing. These days there's no excuse not to have a web presence. Clients, especially those new to town, often find a new salon via Yelp reviews and through online searches. Putting together a website is a minor investment that when done properly has a solid rate of return. Having an active Facebook page and/or Twitter account for the salon is easy, very effective and free. If you search the salon online and there are no reviews, no website, and no web presence—move on.

Knowing how long the stylists have been working at a salon can tell you one of two things. Either they love it there, or there's a contract preventing them from leaving. How do you know? Well, when you ask about contracts, get specific, don't be afraid. This is your future. If there is a contract, find out how far the contract extends to. Some salons specify that a stylist cannot work within three miles of the salon if they choose to leave. Others have a ten or more mile radius. Three miles makes some sense. Ten plus miles? Be wary. These stylists couldn't work anywhere near where they are now, greatly influencing their decision to stay. Personally, I'm not anti-contract, but I would never sign a contract with more than a three mile radius. Contracts with such restrictive terms put off bad vibes, create abuse of power and can foster bitterness in employees. Most hairdressers are going to tell you not to sign a contract at all, but sometimes it can't be avoided. In fact, the only people wanting you to sign a contract are the people who want to sue you if you break it. The fact is they are trying to protect their business. Still, you should be wary of a highly restrictive contract. Sometimes they make sense, and are necessary. Sometimes they can seriously impede a stylist's potential. We'll discuss contracts more in depth in the next chapter.

Conversely, a salon with no contract and a high turnover rate is a warning sign as well. Why do stylists leave or get fired? It's okay to ask the owner or manager why they've let apprentices or stylists go in the past. Ask them why they believe stylists have left their salon. Listen carefully to their answers. You may feel nervous asking these questions. Just remember, this is your future, and there's no shame in gathering as much knowledge as you can about your potential work space. A professional salon owner will understand and respect your inquiries. If anything, it shows attention to detail and thoughtful decision making—two key traits of any successful, professional stylist.

It may shock you to discover many salons pay their apprentices minimum wage. Minimum wage is only acceptable if you are also getting tipped out a guaranteed amount each day. Minimum wage, depending on where you live, can currently range from $4.00 to $10.00 per hour. After taxes, a forty-hour work week would leave you with a paycheck ranging between $120.00 - $275.00 per week. That is hardly enough to live on properly.

I have an issue with paying apprentices minimum wage. Minimum wage is one way of saying "I'm going to pay you the least amount of money allowed by law." Remember, you've invested in yourself by going to cosmetology school. You may or may not have student loans to pay, but you have a right to quality of life. You're educated, you've worked hard through school, you want to learn from the best and deserve to be treated fairly. Why isn't minimum wage fair? Here's why: many apprenticeships run about a year in length. And I have witnessed apprentices get paid minimum wage, with no tip out from the stylists—expected to fold every towel, wash every head, blow dry every client, apply every color—work so hard, yet barely make enough money get by. Basically, they get taken advantage of, and they lose enthusiasm. Some give up and stop pursuing their career during the apprentice process. It's a shame and I don't want that to happen to you. If you do agree to minimum wage, do so *only* if you're guaranteed tips. Your mentor is making good money thanks to you and your assistance. You deserve proper pay.

Your apprenticeship will not be glamorous. There are expectations of the apprentice/assistant that make you essentially a glorified one-man cleaning crew. You will fold towels—lots of them. (If your salon has a towel service, be very thankful.) You will empty trash cans. You will wash more color bowls and bottles and brushes than you ever thought possible. You will sweep a ton of hair. You will get coffee for clients and coffee for your mentor. Make sure to grab a cup for yourself too because you're going to need it. You will stack magazines, wipe countertops, clean stations, possibly unpack retail, replace toilet paper rolls, grab lunch for the crew (don't expect a proper lunch break, by the way) and you'll often shampoo clients for members of the salon team who are in a bind, and they may or may not remember to say thank you or tip you out. Apprenticing is time to learn how a salon is run and a time to participate in team work to an exhausting level. It is grunt work; it is not always fun. You will never sit down. Ever. Your feet will hurt, your back will ache. Your arms will burn from shampooing and blowing out so many heads of hair. It is all part of the salon experience and the reality of being a hairdresser.

That's why length of apprenticeship and specifics regarding the training are also essential questions. Without a guideline as to how long your apprenticeship could last, you could find yourself assisting for longer than necessary. A good mentor will give you a timeline, goals, and clear expectations. Many mentors require their apprentices to perform certain hair color and cutting techniques before 'going on the floor.' This makes sense and is a desirable scenario. A good mentor will also explain haircuts to you as they are doing them—explaining in detail the 'little things' that matter when cutting hair. Often it's what you don't cut that can make or break a hairstyle. Even a half inch has an impact. He or she should also explain their reasons behind their techniques in hair cutting and color. A good mentor will educate you in the salon and provide educational opportunities and hands-on classes outside of the salon as well. Color formulas should also be thoroughly explained. Most apprentices mix color for their mentors. But a good mentor will be there beside you, explaining the ratio and reasons behind the color selection, etc. Apprentices are often expected and trusted to apply color retouches and all over color for their mentors. This is great practice not only in color application, but in learning how to talk with clients naturally, learning about different hair textures, and how much color is typically needed for an application. Time is money, so speed is built up this way. Color is also money, so too much color can cost the salon unnecessary expense. Too little color can cost the stylist valuable time in going back and mixing up a fresh batch. All these details matter. Your time as an apprentice teaches you these often unthought-of scenarios and realities.

When you bring a hair model into the salon for practice, your mentor should allow you to formulate the hair color you wish to use on your model—with guidance of course. Any necessary changes should be advised and the reasons explained. That's how you learn. Develop the habit of writing down every formula you use while you're apprenticing. Often hairstylists get too busy to write formulas down, thinking they will get to it later, or remember the formula regardless. Sometimes this works. You *will* get to the point where you can look at a head of hair and know what needs to be used. But do not rely on this technique. Color fades, hair changes, and even a minuscule amount of a color can make a huge difference in your end result. Clients pay professionals for consistency. If they wanted to play a guessing game they would do their color at home, for a fraction of the price.

When you're cutting a model's hair, your mentor should be attentive to what you're doing so they can correct and guide you as you go. Any mistakes you make should be explained and fixed promptly. Ideally they will not allow you to make such mistakes, but gently guide you and question your motives as your haircut is progressing. It is common to need guidance during your haircuts; don't be afraid or ashamed or too proud to ask for and accept any and all advice. It's different in a salon than it is in cosmetology school. In school, your instructor is there to check your haircut after completion; mistakes are an expected part of the learning curve. In a salon the bar is raised, and your mentor should walk you through the steps initially, giving you tips that make a huge difference. Look at it as they've 'got your back.' As you progress in your training, a simple check at the end of the style is common and it's a sign you're about ready for the floor.

A bit of advice when you're performing services on the floor—whether it's color or haircutting, do not be afraid, and if you do lose your way, don't panic. Take a deep breath and give yourself a moment to reconfigure the haircut. While hair is certainly not rocket science, it is difficult to master properly and build the confidence to do so. Again this is where an apprenticeship is ideal. Confidence is built, and confidence is key. Technique is perfected, communication skills are developed—and communication is the first thing stylists need in order to succeed. Without proper communication—regardless of what school you attended, your apprenticeship, or other training—the odds of leaving a client unsatisfied are fairly high. So, take your time, ask questions, and most importantly talk to your client. It's what hairdressers do all day... think and perform masterpieces all while carrying on a conversation. Most artists require quiet and isolation when crafting their work. We don't have that option. So, use these tips to aid you in your path to finding the best salon for your apprenticeship, use your time wisely, and I promise you will be well on your way to success in the salon industry.

4
CONTRACTS
The Legend of the Salon Non-Compete Agreement

> "Maybe I'm old-school, but I always thought you honor a contract."
> ~ Brett Favre

Should you or shouldn't you sign a contract? This is a divisive topic in the salon industry—salon owners want to protect themselves and their salons; hairstylists want the freedom to work anywhere they choose at any moment of their choosing.

If you were to ask a majority of established hairdressers if you should sign a contract, they would tell you "No." If you were to ask that same group if they've ever signed a contract before, they would most likely tell you "Yes."

It's a tough topic. On one hand, let's say you've spent five years building a clientele at Salon A. An opportunity arises for you to open your own place next door, or perhaps to work with your friend around the corner. Is it ethical to take the clients you acquired from Salon A next door to Salon B or C? This is where a contract comes into play. A contract, also known as a non-compete agreement, protects salon owners from this type of scenario.

It's important to look at the salon owners' and the employees' perspective on this delicate matter, so let's examine both.

Most contracts stipulate if a stylist leaves a salon, they are required to work outside of a certain radius from the current salon for a specified amount of time. This is typically three to five miles and the time frame is usually six months to a year. (Anything over this radius or time frame is a sign of caution and I would highly advise not signing any contract that restricting.) The legality of non-compete contracts varies from state to state, but if you choose to sign a contract assume it will hold up in court.

Of course not all salons have non-competes. Obviously, booth renters and independent contractors would never be required to sign a non-compete. They are typically found only in commission-based salons, hourly-pay salons and chains.

Though they're not the end of the world, think very carefully before you sign a contract, and if something seems wrong to you, don't do it. Follow your gut, and also have a neutral party read over the contract for you. I personally think it's a wise investment to pay a lawyer to read and explain the non-compete to you thoroughly before you sign. If the salon you're looking into working for will not allow you to take a copy of the contract for review, absolutely do not go and work there. A good employer will be comfortable with this and will encourage you to protect yourself. A bad employer will want you to remain uninformed and naïve.

Here's the deal. Salons that spend a significant amount of money promoting their business, educating their staff, and offer a generous pay scale or commission base cannot afford to do so if their stylists are continually leaving for another salon. They invest in advertising, products, and in you personally through training, proper pay, marketing and opportunity for growth. Some salons also offer health insurance coverage or compensation. There are stylists who take advantage of an employer's investment in them, and in absence of a contract, use a salon to build their client base then take their clients and run. This hardly seems fair to the employer and is a serious threat to small independently-owned hair salons. This industry has a high turnover rate, and some stylists just aren't mature enough—and never will be—to understand the business side of investing in your own salon. Salon owners take a huge risk initially, and having a revolving door can potentially ruin their business. So before you sign a contract, or choose not to sign one, it's important to go back to step one... which is, take your time choosing the salon that's right for you before you make a commitment or sign any agreement. Once an agreement is signed you need to honor its terms and conditions. Regardless of a contract or not, the good news is most clients follow their stylist to a new location. Once a client is in a stylist's chair, it's the stylist who is the deciding factor on if the client will return or not. A salon's name or reputation may get clients in the door, but you're the one who keeps them there. A handful may stay salon loyal for a myriad of reasons—but the majority of clients want to stay with you if they are happy with the way you do their hair. If a client loves their stylist they will follow. If a client loves the salon they will stay with the salon. Before signing a contract with a salon, make sure you understand fully what the contract specifies, and then honor that contract should you decide to leave. The most important thing you can do is to be a professional. That is how you build your clientele, and avoid burning professional bridges. You want to be able to focus on your clients when you're working, not focused on a legal battle should you break a contract with your employer by leaving. It's okay to sign a contract if you must— just be sure to do so intelligently.

Now let's take a moment to further examine the perspective of the salon owner. If you're a commissioned or salaried employee at a salon it's important to understand the business from an owner's point of view. Believe it or not, when I asked salon owners if given the choice to go back in time and do things differently, nearly half said they would choose *not* to open their own salon again. Needless to say, I was a bit shocked.

Every salon owner I know loves their occupation; they must, or else they wouldn't be able to handle the pressures of salon ownership. They love hair and design and people and stay in the business for the same reasons we all do. It's incredibly creative, fun, and fulfilling. Unfortunately, there often is a huge gap of understanding between stylists and stylist owners. Why is that, and how can we prevent this separation between salon owner and staff? Consider this— all salon owners were (most likely) once employees of a salon, either salary based or commission. They had a vision of a better work environment for themselves and for others, and they built upon that dream by opening their own salon. Having never owned a business before, the first years of owning your own salon bring with them huge learning curves. Staff often come and go until they find the right team. The initial overhead and start up investment can be significant, depending on salon size and location. Leases are signed, commitments are made, and nerves are shot while dreams are being pursued. Owning your own salon takes a huge amount of time, money and faith. Once the learning curve is over, salon owners go from "building" mode into protective mode, determined to keep their business thriving. They barely have time to breathe and enjoy what they've created because running a salon is an endeavor that goes way beyond a normal work day.

As a salon employee, I've witnessed massive employee walkouts, heard tales of and felt the after-effects of employee theft, have seen stylists and receptionists fail to show up for work; all scenarios that directly affected my day and business. Imagine owning the salon that has to weather these predicaments?

I'm not talking about owning a chain salon, where the owners are out of sight and typically not even hairstylists, or an individual suite or loft, where it's one stylist working solo. I'm talking about running an independently owned, vital to our community, local kick-ass hair salon. The type of salon many stylists imagine working in. We all have a vision in our head of our dream place to work. And then we think we've found it or built it, only to realize nothing is perfect. This is where the gap between stylist and salon owner exists. I think as visual and tactile creative human beings, we often seek perfection in places it cannot exist. Because we want our clients' hair to be perfect, and we do that to the best of our abilities, we think our workplace should be perfect too.

Owning a salon and working in a salon requires the owner and employee practice compassion, mutual respect and understanding of each other, and it also demands hard work and dedication to the team. You must be a unified front. Ideally a salon owner will have business management experience, but many don't. They are creative spirits, going out on a limb and running their own space. And thank god they do. Independent salons are found at the epicenter of every community, and bring necessary energy and style, as well as employment to their neighborhood.

Let's go even deeper into salon owner responsibilities. Unless they employ a specific salon manager, salon owners are the manager. This means they are responsible for numerous administrative tasks, such as ordering products, keeping track of inventory and stock, replenishing supplies, paying bills, meeting with distributors, hiring staff, handling computer issues, fielding sales reps, customer complaints, staff complaints, and so on and so forth. They also must deal with issues such as theft and loss of income due to no-shows. They monitor costs, work on promotions, deal with economic fluctuations, maintain and promote a website, research the latest training and education, figure payroll and taxes, while continuously maintaining and selling an image.

Salon owners are also responsible for finding an excellent front desk receptionist, which is one of the hardest jobs in a salon to fill. Until online booking completely takes over client bookings, the front desk is vital to a salon's success. Many salon owners I've talked to said filling this position was one of the most frustrating aspects of their job. The front desk handles many of your client relations in addition to your money. You have to be able to trust your front desk staff completely.

Additionally, many salon owners employ an assistant or apprentice not only to help them keep on schedule, but with the promise they will mentor them properly towards success in the salon business.

All of this, on top of their number one priority, which is taking care of their clients properly.

Keep this in mind when dealing with any issues that may arise between you and your salon owner. Independent salons provide a necessary retreat within a community. While work options are bountiful in our industry, a world full of only booth rental salons and individual salon suites limits the options not only for stylists but for clients and the community as well, and unless we make a conscious effort to respect and understand each other within the salon industry, small independent salons could become a rarity, and that would be devastating to our industry. Remember that diversity, options, and freedom are qualities hair salons and hair stylists symbolize via the nature of the work we do and the community we serve.

Of course, there will always be circumstances where a salon owner has found themselves in over their head. Some people really shouldn't run a business or manage people. It's understandable to not want to work in such a scenario, and a contract can force you to stay in an improperly managed work environment. Stylists who are treated poorly by their employers have every right to find a new place to work. A contract with ridiculous boundaries (over five miles or one year) almost forces the stylist to stay where he or she is, even when they're unhappy. It's unfortunate, but some salon owners treat their contract-bound staff terribly.

Here are a few examples of what would be considered poor treatment, contract or not:

- Being taken advantage of—required to work extra for no pay. (Obviously, volunteer and educational opportunities are the exception.)

- No room or opportunity for income growth (your pay or commission stays the same regardless of your service totals.)

- No education or educational incentives.

- No open communication or, the fear of retribution if you try to bring your concerns to the employer and or management.

- Consistent mistakes being made regarding your clientele, appointment scheduling, or paycheck.

- An unclean, unsanitary work environment or an unstable environment where basic needs are vulnerable (such as water, electricity, etc. due to negligence.)

- Any purposeful malicious intent.

As a stylist, you also have a responsibility to treat your workplace, salon owner, and coworkers with respect, recognizing it takes proper, positive management *and* teamwork to run a successful, professional salon. This type of harmony between a salon owner and stylist makes for the ultimate win-win situation. Below are a few basic "dos and don'ts" stylists can follow to make the workplace run smoother for all.

DO:

Show up for work, and show up on time. (Sounds simple, right?) Many salon owners listed stylists not showing up, or—just as bad—stylists showing up late, as their number one annoyance. I believe it's ideal to arrive at the salon twenty to thirty minutes before your first appointment, so you can prepare for your day before your first client walks through the door.

Help out when you can. Be kind and attentive to all the clients in the salon, not just yours. If you see someone who looks lost, ask how you can be of service. If you notice a client needs help or assistance, be there for them. If you see a fellow stylist in need of an extra pair of hands, offer yours to them. It's about projecting and creating a team work environment, where we all look out for eachother.

Be professional. If your salon has a dress code, follow it. If it doesn't, make sure you still dress professionally. It's possible (and encouraged!) for hairdressers to express their personalities while still maintaining a professional appearance. (More on this in chapter nine.)

Understand that not every day is going to go according to schedule or plan. Occasional mistakes happen, its human nature. Power outages happen, that's Mother Nature. You have to be able to adjust your day and attitude accordingly.

DON'T:

Backstab in the break room. Gossip, whether it's about

another stylist or your employer or the front desk, will only negatively affect you in the end.

Assume. If you're questioning any part of your book or paycheck, go directly to your employer to work it out. If you feel you're not receiving new clients as often as others, again, go directly to your employer to discuss.

Forget that owning a salon takes an incredible amount of energy. For every benefit your employer brings to you, there is a cost. So before you sign on at any salon, remember, if there's healthcare, education, supplies, marketing, and so forth involved, your commission rate will be affected. This should all be discussed prior to joining any salon team.

I believe if a salon treats their staff properly and professionally, there is no need for a non-compete contract, but I respect a salon owner's desire to protect their investment via a non-compete. Sounds contradictory, but in a perfect world non-competes wouldn't exist; however, this is not a perfect world so they do. I do believe salons can and should create an environment their stylists want to remain loyal to. Stylists who are happy with their employer, and who are treated properly, typically do not want to salon-hop—unless they have ambitions to open their own space or absolutely must adjust their work environment to suit their personal needs best.

My hope is for you to never find yourself stuck somewhere because of an overly restrictive contract, that you choose the salon to work with carefully, that you never experience mistreatment by your employer, and that you treat with respect all of those you spend your work day with.

5
INTERVIEW: SALON OWNER/STYLIST ANGELA PACKER
She Puts the Pro in Professional

"The only place success comes before work is in the dictionary." ~ Vince Lombardi

Angela and I go way back—we've worked together twice in our careers, which for both of us began during the early nineties. I've learned so much from Angela over the years. She's an impeccable hairstylist. She defines no-nonsense. You want precision? You want a true professional you can trust? Well, then you probably already go to Angela at the salon she co-owns with her business partner, Chris.

You've been a hairdresser now for twenty-two years... What do you enjoy the most about being a hairstylist?

I like so much about it. I actually really liked it when I was a

receptionist. I was sixteen. I liked the music. I liked how the hairstylists dressed. I loved the attitude. Very fun, very social, so I loved that. That's why I went to hair school. Now, I'd say I pretty much love it because I love the people. My clients. I love them. And they love me. Certainly they love me because of my craft, and what I'm able to do for them bleeds over into how they feel about me, and that leaves me feeling completely fulfilled. There's a lot of love in the hair salon.

We have a very similar story. I began as a receptionist too, and fell in love with the entire scene.

Oh my God. New Order. Bizarre Love Triangle. What else was there?

No doubt. I think music, and the creativity it inspires, is one of the reasons I became a hairstylist. Fast forwarding a bit, what do you wish you knew about the business when you decided to open your salon?

How to run a business. I wish I knew how to effectively get a loan in order to not go into copious amounts of personal debt when we were opening the salon; taking a business course in order to know how to run a salon. I've learned that when the learning curve is as you're doing it, it's going to be rougher and steeper than say if you had gone about it properly—with a proper loan and a business course as opposed to running it based how you feel—going on pure emotion.

So, in your experience, a lot of hairstylists aren't

necessarily business people, but many desire to run their own salons, and are usually 'good with people,' but that's not enough.

Right. And if you're running a business you should have specific business skills... be business oriented because managing finances, and bills, and stock, is very different than managing people—emotions and personalities and wants and needs. Two totally different sets of skills. That's what I wish I knew when I was starting in the business, and definitely before I opened my salon.

I feel there's often a sense of disconnect between the stylist as salon owner and the stylist as employee.

I think part of the feeling of disconnect is because it's kind of like being out on the field as opposed to being the coach. When you're on the field you're looked at as a team player, part of the team. When you're the coach you're not viewed as one of the team-mates. It's a totally different approach and perspective at work each day. For example, if a stylist mixes four ounces of color for their client, but only uses half of it, and puts the rest down the drain, that's a problem for me. They're literally throwing money away. Not to mention the environmental effect of color going down the drain. But as a salon owner I have to watch our expenses and keep our costs reigned in, in order for everyone to make money; yet the moment I say something about color being wasted or what not I'm the mean guy.

What advice would you give a current cosmetology

student?

Your image is everything. Learn that now. You're going to be judged immediately upon how you look. If you have piercings and you have tattoos, I think that is industry-wide acceptable, however that is not acceptable to a conservative clientele. So know your market and know what image you want to present professionally. Choose a salon that fits your image, but be willing to adapt to your environment if need be.

Also, perfect your craft. For example, if you want to be the best haircutter or colorist, take every class you can, continuously, so that you're constantly upping your game. Totally own that.

Be an apprentice. You're not going to make much money initially, but if you want this I think being an apprentice is essential.

You've mentored stylists. What do you look for in an apprentice?

I can help train someone to do great hair, but I can't train someone to be a nice person. So, I look for nice people. I look for people who are problem solvers, and who have a willingness and desire to learn. I look for someone who likes people. I can't train someone to be happy, or in a good mood, or to want to be there, so... I look for nice people. And I never ask my apprentice to do something I wouldn't do. I respect them, and in return I expect them to respect me.

Any advice you'd like to share with stylists new to the business?

Always make eye contact. Be respectful—you can be funny, you can be raunchy, you can be whoever you are and still be respectful. Learn how to read a persons (your clients) mood, and then be aware and respectful of that as well. And one of the worst things I see stylists do is engage with their co-workers when there's a client sitting in their chair. If you engage the client with your co-workers and conversation, that's fine... but if you're having way too much fun talking you're not paying attention to your client, your job—you're not cutting the hair properly, you're not doing what they're expecting you to do, and you can lose your clients trust. Pay attention to your clients.

As always, it's been real. Thanks for meeting me for lunch. Any other words of wisdom you'd like to share?

In this business, you make lifelong friends—both with co-workers and clients, but especially with many of your co-workers. I think about each and every person I've worked with or have had as a client quite often. And here we are, twenty years after first working together, having lunch. It's amazing.

.

6
YOUR FIRST YEAR AS A HAIRSTYLIST
Building a Clientele

"Being good in business is the most fascinating kind of art. Making money is art and working is art and good business is the best art.
~ Andy Warhol

You've graduated from cosmetology school, completed a proper and (hopefully) educational and inspiring apprenticeship, and now you're going "on the floor."

Finally, you'll do some hair and make some money!

Think again.

I don't mean to discourage—quite the opposite. I want you to be fully informed so you are prepared for your career. The first years as a hairdresser are tough. Depending on the salon you're in, building a clientele could be somewhat painless, or it could be a challenge. This is why researching before you choose a salon is essential. It's also why it's important to visualize where you want to be long term with your career. Obviously, if you choose a walk-in chain style salon you will have customers (not clients, there's a difference) right away. If you choose a large high volume upscale salon or spa, you will also build rather quickly (due to salon name recognition, marketing, and the sheer volume of customers large salons often appeal to.) Both types of salons have their cons that can be equal to or greater than their pros, so weigh your decision carefully and explore all your options before you commit. Small, independently owned salons often cannot afford to market themselves in the same way as a chain or spa, or afford the rent in high traffic areas (promoting walk-ins)—they often rely on word-of-mouth and the stylists have to hustle. So if you're in a smaller independent salon, it will take more time to build, but you will often build a more loyal clientele in this type of salon. Why? Because word-of-mouth referrals and client-centered individualized customer care are the secret to your success.

It can be discouraging no matter where you work, to spend the day at the salon and only have one or two clients. You will question why you ever became a stylist. You will dream of money and tips and clients pre-booking. On some days you will still feel like an assistant—helping those who are more established. You may grow bitter—don't. Regardless of the salon you're working in, attracting and building your clientele is up to you.

Once a client is in a salon, and then in your chair—it is your job to make them want to return, and most importantly, return to you. It's a lot of pressure and responsibility— remember to stay calm and confident. Take your time, ask the important questions, and always keep in mind that people like getting their hair done. You're not a dentist or oncologist—you're a hairdresser. People look forward to seeing you. You help them look and feel their best. It really is a unique, honorable and fun profession.

Before you begin any hair service on a first-time client, here are the Important Questions:

- About how much time do you spend on your hair each day?

- Do you blow dry or style your hair every day? (Get specific—do you use a vent brush, a round brush, a diffuser...) Show them the different brushes and tools so they know exactly what you're asking.

- Do you curl or flat iron your hair often?

- What styling products do you use, and do you like the results they give you?

- What do wish your hair to look like but have been told it can't do?

- What about your hair really bothers you? (People often can relay what they don't like about their hair easier than expressing what they do like.)

- What about your hair do you love? (It's important to help them find the positive qualities they already possess.)

- Did you bring any pictures to share with me? (If not, grab a few magazines or use your smartphone and flip through photos with them—pointing out what will work, some ideas you had in mind, what should be avoided... ask them to show you pictures they like, and pictures they do not like at all. Then, ask them why. You'll learn a lot this way.)

Remember that your enthusiasm and attention to detail will automatically put most clients at ease. These are a lot of questions, and really they're just a start. As your conversation begins to flow naturally you'll think of more questions to ask depending on your client's response. Reassure them you have their best interest in mind with these questions—many people, unfortunately, have never experienced a hairdresser who takes their time before the haircut begins to find out this vital (and often fun) information. It's the beginning of your bonding time with your client. You might as well get used to talking with people now—while you're building your clientele and have the time and flexibility to do so. As your eye, skill, ability to read body language, and experience builds, this consultation will still take place—but your intuition and knowledge will answer many questions for you. The first year is the time to strengthen those traits.

Good communication skills are *vital* to success in our industry. As hairstylists, our words are very powerful. People listen to us and take our advice on how to look and feel their best. They trust us. So therefore it is important to be upfront and honest with a client during the consultation. This is hard for many stylists, both new and experienced. We want to be honest about our abilities, but we don't want to look incompetent in any way, and at our core we are people pleasers in every way. If you're in a consultation, and your client wants a look that you know will not suit their hair type, or a color that will not work with their skin tone or commitment level, it is of utmost importance that you tell them what they desire will not work, and give them the reasons why. Your gut will tell you when you should not do a particular style or color on someone. Listen to it—for if you make a promise to deliver a result that cannot be achieved or maintained properly, your client will blame you, lose faith in your ability, and move on to another stylist. It's hard for us to say no. But I promise you this—if you say no, and they find someone else to do what they want and it goes as predicted—you're the professional, intelligent hairdresser and the other person is to blame. If you say yes, and the results are as you predicted, you're the one at fault. On top of that, people tend to complain more than praise. So if a client leaves your chair unhappy (as your gut may have cautioned) they will tell more people about their negative experience than they would if you said no. On the contrary, giving people a look that both suits them and looks beautiful will bring referrals into your chair, and that's the ultimate goal for a hairdresser. Positive word-of-mouth coupled with beautiful results is the best way to build a lasting clientele.

While styling their hair let them know what products you are using and why—and never with the sole intention of selling them a product to up your retail commission (though that's nice if you receive one). I feel it's important to use products you believe in and are educated on. I also believe it's our job as hairstylists to educate our clients about the benefits of using salon quality hair care. If possible, give your clients samples to take home and use. Often they will realize your professional recommendations really can make a difference in how their hair looks and feels. Plus, it shows you really do care about the integrity of their hair.

When you're finished with your service and your client both looks and feels amazing, I recommend you always walk with your client to the front desk. It's also a good idea to give them several of your cards. I recommend at least three. Let them know you appreciate referrals, and consider offering a discount to clients who send their friends your way. This is a great way to build your clientele. I gave my clients ten percent off their service any time they referred someone to me, not just when I was a new stylist. Clients love feeling appreciated, and we need to never take their belief in us for granted.

If you happen to be on Facebook or Twitter (or any of the social media sites) I highly recommend inviting your clients to follow you online after their service is complete. We'll dive into using social media to build and inspire your clientele thoroughly in chapter fourteen.

I also highly recommend you follow-up with first time clients with a thank-you note, sent to them the old fashioned way—snail mail. Writing a personal, handwritten note may seem a bit archaic and frankly foreign to some, but it is a very personal and genuine way to express your gratitude. And, since we are in the business of personal beauty, a handwritten letter is merely an extension of the conversation you held with your client while they were in your styling chair. Here's an example of what this note could look like:

Dear Beyoncé,

It was a pleasure meeting you last week. I hope you are enjoying your new haircut (color, etc... whatever service they experienced with you). I look forward to seeing you again, ideally in 4-6 weeks to keep your hair looking great. Be sure to call Mariah at the front desk (555-555-5555) to schedule your next appointment, if you haven't done so already. Thank you so much. In the meantime, if you have any further hair questions, need products, or your bangs trimmed—you know where to find me!

Sincerely,
Your Awesome Hairstylist

(Remember to place a few business cards in with your note so Beyoncé can pass them on to her friends!)

While we're on the subject of personal correspondence, there are a few other times in your career when a personal letter seems fit. When (and if) you decide to move to a new salon, when a client has been overly generous sending referrals to you, and when you realize you haven't seen a once regular client in your chair for quite some time. (Later, in chapter 19, is where you will find a sample letter to a client for when you change salons.) When a client has sent multiple clients your way, sending them a personal thank-you takes only a few minutes of your time, yet shows your appreciation in a very sincere way. At a time when the majority of quick correspondence often happens via text messages and emails, receiving an unexpected thank-you letter in the mail can make someone's day.

The more difficult letter to write is when you haven't seen a client for a period of time. Of course, you don't need to reach out to them—all of this is purely your choice. And let's be frank—there will be instances when a client leaves and you will find yourself quite relieved. But there will be moments when the absence of a once regular client leaves you with an unsettled feeling. For those times, there is no harm or shame in reaching out to them—it actually shows you care, that you notice their absence, and that they are important to you. There are many reasons for a client to leave their stylist. Some reasons are simple, others more complicated. I recommend you not insist on knowing why they left—instead focus on the fact you notice their absence and hope all is well. Here's an example letter for this delicate time:

Dear Beyoncé,

I haven't seen you in the salon recently, and wanted to reach out to let you know you've been missed! If there's anything I can do to be of service to you again, please don't hesitate to call. I've always enjoyed having you in my chair, and I hope this letter finds you well.

Sincerely,
Your Starting-To-Worry-But-Still-Awesome Hairstylist

Include your business card with this correspondence, and consider offering a ten percent discount on their next service with you as well. You never know—sometimes people leave because they can no longer afford your services, and they don't know how to say that. Sometimes an incident occurs in the salon that you are unaware of, and this letter gives them the opportunity to reach out to you so you can make it right. The point is, if a client's absence doesn't quite make sense and leaves you concerned, you should reach out to that client.

There is a lot to learn in this business, the technical part being a mere fraction compared to mastering the communication, professional and interpersonal relationship, and business building skills that are all equally necessary. Above all, work hard and remember the first year is all about patience, practice, self-promotion, perseverance and staying positive.

7
WHAT CLIENTS LOOK FOR IN A SALON AND STYLIST
Words of Wisdom From the Client's Perspective

"Life is an endless struggle full of frustrations
and challenges, but eventually you find a
hairstylist that understands you."
~ Author unknown

Here's the deal. People really enjoy getting their hair cut.
They look forward to it. If you can provide a relaxing
environment and instill a sense of trust, your client will
return to you. The current trends in the beauty industry are
salons that look and feel a bit like home. The big, glossy,
over-the-top salon is somewhat losing fashion. People crave
intimacy and community. They enjoy the unique
atmosphere and culture that smaller salons provide. They
feel that when they're in a one-of-a-kind space, they're

receiving a one-of-a-kind style. It's a salon that's warm and personable, where organic conversation seems to flow more naturally. The mood is stylish, yet comforting. Intimate, yet edgy. Modern, yet warm.

Of course, salon size and feeling won't matter one bit if a client isn't pleased with their hair experience. Big salon or small, clients want to feel great when they walk out the door.

When asked what they look for in a salon and stylist, this is what one client had to say:

"When I consider a new hairdresser, I want to know that they work in a salon where they consistently partake in continuing education. I enjoy a stylist who is always willing to try something new and that each of their clients look different from age to age. I also feel like you really need to connect with your hairstylist and have good communication with them."

Here the client has stressed that education is key. She wants her stylist to be on top of his or her game. She believes it is via education that stylists are able to provide fresh hairstyles for their clients. Education is vital to staying relevant in our industry. Not only does it keep you inspired and current, it also validates pay raises, boosts your self-worth and self-esteem. When you attend big hair shows, it's important to take the hands-on (aka break-out) classes. Small classes are the best because you can focus, ask questions, and receive one-on-one guidance. Any time you invest in continuing education, it's important to share what you've learned with your clients. Let them know you're constantly improving your game and learning new things. They will respect your dedication and commitment to your profession, and they will remember your advanced training whenever the times arise that you need to implement a soft price increase. It's important to note, though not quite the same as certified classes, during any down time at work, you can also watch a myriad of tutorials online (which are free and often awesome) and pay close attention to trends as you flip through magazines. Of course stating you watch videos about hair will not justify a price increase or replace formal education, but they can teach you new things and be inspiring.

Next let's take a look at this next client, as she describes how she wants to feel... she wants to be "wowed!"

"I was going to a salon for several years, seeing two different stylists there, and both ladies did a nice job with my hair. But I was never "wowed." Then a girl I worked with suggested her stylist to do a particular hairstyle I saw in a magazine. I went to her stylist and it was the best hairstyle I had ever had! Completely exceeded my expectations. He was intuitive with the cut and color that I wanted, seemed extremely educated, and seemed to just know what I needed. Plus it didn't look horrendous when it grew out."

This is an example of a client who was reasonably satisfied with her stylist(s) but left them in pursuit of a new hairstyle. She felt a new stylist would be able to do a better job. The way to prevent this from happening to you is to treat your clients as if it is the first time they've sat in your chair each and every time, and again—keep up on your education and let your clients know you're up to date and capable of any look. Also, never take a long-standing client for granted by assuming they want the same color or haircut every time. Consult each and every visit. Offer new suggestions. Tweak their current style every so often to prevent boredom (for both of you). Stay on top of fashion and show them pictures of new looks that would work for them if and when they're ready. Encourage them to bring in photos of hair they love. Be open to change, never assume, and stay current. Even if your client comes to you because she loves how consistent you are—you never know. One day she may be thinking she'd like something new, and if she thinks you're only capable of one look or one color for her, she will go elsewhere.

Notice the client's use of the word 'intuitive'. She loved how this new stylist seemed to know just what she needed and wanted. This comes with time. As your career evolves you'll learn how to hear what people are saying in a whole new way. You'll be able to read body language, hand gestures, between the lines, and so much more. You will, in fact, become somewhat psychic when it comes to what a client needs. You will be able to tell them accurately what they want, executing the look perfectly, which is exactly what we get paid top dollar for.

Now here a client emphasizes honesty as the main trait she looks for in a stylist:

"I love a stylist who does what I want or tells me if what I want will not work with my hair. I need to feel like it's okay to tell them if I like what they've done or not as well. Open communication and honesty are key."

Again, communication and connecting with the stylist are both mentioned.

Clients have very simple needs. They desire a stylist who is knowledgeable, friendly, and that listens well but also offers suggestions. They want someone they feel comfortable talking to, can form a connection with, grow with, and trust. When a client sits in your chair for the first time, they feel the same way you mostly likely do—excited and nervous.

Now let's take a moment and focus specifically on some client testimonies regarding how they feel when they go see a stylist for the first time.

"When I go to see a stylist for the first time I usually read reviews online. Overall I'm excited to see a new stylist because he or she can (hopefully) suggest something new for my hair."

"First time with a stylist = Anxiety! I don't know if we will like each other or not, or if he/she will understand my hair and personality."

"Moving to a new city poses two challenges—finding a

new dentist (I'm very particular about my teeth!) and finding a new stylist (I'm even more particular about my hair!) Starting a new relationship with a stylist gives me anxiety. If something goes wrong you can be stuck looking like a fool for weeks! My biggest problem is that I know what I like and dislike, but I have a hard time conveying my thoughts. Finding someone who can read between the lines of my description is key."

Many people compared going to a new stylist for the first time to going on a first date. Overall, when I asked people how they felt, anxiety and nervousness were the top responses. Very few people were nonchalant—and as many men as women expressed their nervousness. I believe the first date analogy is a good one. Ideally, the stylist should feel like he or she is on a first date as well. A new client in your chair is never to be taken for granted. You want to see this person again, and what you do to their hair and the way you treat them defines you as a stylist, and determines whether you'll see them again or not. I've both observed and personally experienced having my hair cut by someone for the first time who seemed to care more about talking than cutting, completely ignoring most if not all of what I desired to have my hair look like. Now I admit, I may be a bit more critical considering hair design and customer service are two of my passions—but if I'm sitting there thinking *this is not how I expected this to go*, I can only imagine how someone outside of the industry must often feel. More importantly, I too have smiled and thanked them, left only partially satisfied, knowing full well I would not be back. And, I didn't speak up. Why is that? Well, it's awkward, that's why.

Take into consideration this testimonial, from a sixty-five-year-old client, who still can recall—thirty years later—her worst salon experience:

"I was thirty five and my youngest child was just a baby. I'd had long, free-flowing, very curly hair since I was a kid. After the baby, though, I was so busy rushing around with the other two kids and working part time.... I decided to be brave and give shorter hair a try. My neighbor had hair similar to mine, so I asked her to recommend someone to help me make a change.

It was a disaster.

When I arrived at the salon, the stylist barely looked me in the eye. I felt like I was interrupting her conversation with the other stylist. She'd had an argument with her boyfriend the night before, and her co-worker was offering advice (bad advice, in my opinion). The stylist did ask me what I had in mind, and I tried to explain—told her how my hair behaves in both dry and humid weather, asked her what hairstyles she thought would work, and that her client (my neighbor) also came to her and that I loved my neighbor's hair and thought texture was similar. We agreed to a cut about six inches shorter than what I was currently wearing.

She began in the back, and I soon realized she was cutting my hair short; significantly shorter than we had discussed. All this time, she's still talking with her friend, such drama....

my instincts told me to just get up and leave. But it was too late. As she got to the front, she cut lots of short layers, leaving me no options—I had a head of ringlet curls and looked like a marshmallow. I felt like crying and I remember thinking, my children aren't going to recognize me. The entire way home I cried. The next day I called another friend and asked her who her stylist was. Luckily her hairdresser could see me that day, and she could at least soften what I referred to as my "clown 'do."

I promised myself that day that if I ever heard a stylist sound angry before I even sat down, I'd leave fast. Also, I learned when making a big change, I'd go in for a consultation first, then proceed forward.

Even my children remember my disastrous haircut. My older daughter remembers being embarrassed for me! My husband, trying to find the bright side, said I had a lot of patience."

Notice how detailed her memory is, of an experience she had thirty years prior, of going to a new stylist and unfortunately having a negative experience? Most people never forget a horrible hair experience. Stop for a second and think about your own hair experiences over the years. What did you recall? I'll guess you remembered two moments—your worst hair, and your best.

Memories of a bad hair experience are hard to let go of. In fact, while doing research for this book, one woman told me her office has a bad haircut support group.

What we do matters. Immensely.

Let's not forget the men. Here's a male perspective on how he feels going to a stylist for the first time:

"I mentally downplay my concern over my hair. I never think it is a big deal UNTIL I'm sitting in the chair and they start cutting. Then I SUDDENLY care about my hair."

Here's another male perspective. He sums his pre-haircut ritual up rather simply:

"I pray. Something from the Old Testament. Samson and all that."

Now I know this man, and he is not the type to pray over just anything. And, if you met him your first impression would be that he's a very confident, intelligent, kind and easygoing man. His height alone—I'd estimate he's around six-foot-four—gives him great presence. You'd never guess he was nervous. Or, that he cared too much. But he is, and he does, and that's very important to remember.

Lots of men downplay their concern. I think that's part of a particular person's personality and part social conditioning. Lots of men think they're not supposed to care that much, or think they should be able to shrug a bad haircut off. I have found all of my male clients to be exactly the opposite. They want to look good, and they don't want to fuss over their hair too much. Just like women.

Here's a testimonial from a fashionable yet down-to-earth

fifty-two-year-old woman who receives color and a haircut every four weeks, plus purchases salon products—a great client to have.

"The qualities I look for in a hair stylist are—artistic, down to earth, mature, other-centered, caring, service-oriented, and makes me feel special."

Here's she goes on to explain why she has left a stylist / salon in the past:

"I have left salons / stylists because the price value seemed out of whack. I felt like I was continuing to get the same service and look each time with no sense of originality yet paying more for it. I have also left stylists who were self-absorbed, shallow and offensive."

Here a client describes what she looks for in a stylist, some of her best and worst experiences, and how she feels about pricing:

"My best salon experiences have always revolved around finding someone who listened to what I needed with both my color and style. My busy lifestyle dictates many of my choices and I need someone who understands that. Who I choose to do my hair is one way (and an important one) I choose to spend my time and money.

My worst experience was going to a well known stylist who dictated every aspect of my hair without consulting me, and then they proceeded to pass me on to their assistant for both the color and haircut. This stylist was constantly tooting his own horn and bad mouthing other salons and hair care companies.

I do believe hair design is an art form; you have to be able to look at the raw material and see it as an unfinished sculpture. As far as pricing goes, it's talent, not cost, that drives me. And there are talented stylists at every price point. Expensive doesn't guarantee quality."

Wow. Read that again. First, she makes it clear that she views her stylist as an investment—how she spends her time and money. She also remembers a horror story, where the stylist was unprofessional on many levels (no consultation, ignoring her, and gossiping). But the last paragraph is the killer—she views hair design as art. She respects and admires a good hairdresser. And she lets you know that quality is not always equal to cost. She pays top dollar for talent. A better person could most likely do her hair for her at a lower price, if need be.

8
PRICING YOUR SERVICES
Knowing When, Why and How to Increase Your Prices

"You don't get paid for the hour. You get paid for the value you bring to the hour."
~ Jim Rohn

Time is money. My cosmetology instructor repeated that to us daily, and in the salon industry it is the truth. I'd like to further expand on this mantra to include time equals money and money equals energy.

Pricing your salon services, whether you're a salon owner, an independent contractor, or commissioned employee, can be stressful and intimidating. Regardless of where you live and the type of salon you're in, how do you know what your time is worth and how to charge accordingly? Your prices are a reflection of your talent, dedication, education, time, energy, and expertise. What's the big difference between a ten-dollar haircut and a hundred-dollar haircut, some may ask? A twenty-dollar color and a seventy-dollar color? The answer is attention to detail, experience, and the value you place on your time.

You've chosen to become a hairstylist and you should be proud of your profession. In the beginning of your career, you can expect your prices to be on the lower end of the scale, and that will vary greatly depending on where you've chosen to work—both geographically and the type of salon you've chosen. Over time, you will increase your prices as your business, education and experience grow. You should set goals for yourself, knowing hard work and dedication will lead to financial success in our industry.

The beginning of your career is a time to hone your skills, find your groove, practice the art of talking naturally with people from all walks of life, and fine-tune the art of listening. You can expect to start at the low end and gradually move up. You are charging less money in exchange for experience. Eventually, the coin will flip, and people will pay you more money for the experience you've acquired. So how do you know when it's time to raise your prices?

Raising one's prices can be scary. You're finally booked consistently. You're comfortable with clients and gaining more confidence in your talent. You're working much harder, and know quite a bit more than you did in the beginning. You've invested money into better equipment and education. You're putting in forty hours a week with little or no down time and this has made your income increase but you find yourself not quite satisfied. You want to increase your prices but you're afraid clients will leave you after you've worked so hard to secure your base clientele…

These feelings are normal and every hairdresser experiences them. When you've reached this point remember this—time equals money and money equals energy. You've hit the point where your energy has been expanded to its maximum capacity, and you are not receiving the same amount of energy (in the form of money in this case) back in return. If you stay in this zone, your chances of burning out significantly increase. As I've said before you should be proud of your work and your profession. Most corporate positions reward their employees with periodic raises for their hard work. Why shouldn't you receive a raise for your hard work as well? Some salons have a scale with goals attached, paving the way for your proper income advancement. Other salons leave that decision up to the stylist. And if you're in booth rental or independent contracting, pricing decisions are left entirely up to you.

Know this—you will lose a few clients. You'll lose the ones who try to get the most for the least amount of money. But you will keep the majority of your clientele. You may not believe that when it's time to make the decision to increase your prices, because fear will take over. But fear will not pay your bills, increase your quality of life, advance your career, or play a positive role in your self-esteem and self-worth.

Fear will keep you from growing. Fear will keep you from realizing your full potential, fulfilling your dreams, and opening new doors. The clients that leave will go to the stylists that are priced below you, until they too raise their prices. Look at them as part of the salon industry food chain. New stylists need clients, and that's what the price-conscious clients are there for. It all works, because every level stylist has a clientele that's suited for them.

Most clients, once they find someone they like, will stick with their stylist for many years, and they expect your prices to increase over time. The only time I've heard clients express negativity in regards to their stylist increasing their prices, is when the consistency and service are not in line with the price increase. One client shared with me the following observation:

"I had been going to my stylist for quite some time and every year or so her prices would increase. I understood why and was happy initially to pay her prices. However, it seemed over time she was constantly running late, quit consulting with me before she began my haircut, and in general it seemed she did not value my time although I certainly valued hers. I left because I felt I was being taken advantage of. As her prices increased I felt her quality decreased. It no longer made sense to pay for her services."

There's a lot to explore here. She clearly stated she felt taken advantage of. After all, she had demonstrated that she valued her stylist's time by agreeing to pay more, but the stylist did not reciprocate this same feeling by her actions—making her client wait too long, not consulting with her, etc... When you raise your prices you are also raising your standards and your clients' expectations. Many stylists find it necessary to hire an assistant once they hit a certain level of 'traffic' in their salon or chair. Assistants are valuable in helping us stay on time and in assisting us in taking the best care of our clients. A good assistant is worth every penny and should be treated as such. What a stylist with an assistant should never do is assume. I've seen many stylists send their assistant to get their next client and shampoo them, and/or apply their color—without ever personally greeting and talking to their client. This is a huge mistake, and that client will most likely leave you. They may want to change their look or consult with you, as they should and you should expect. To be a successful stylist who brings in a good income and is deserving of higher pricing, you need to treat each client with the same amount of attention and respect as if it were their first time in your chair or else they will feel neglected and unimportant—especially as your prices increase. Just keep that in mind as your career advances. When you are paid properly for your time, you respect yourself more, which attracts clients who respect you and your time as well.

It is of utmost importance to inform your clientele that you will be raising your prices prior to the increase taking effect. Some salons word this as a 'promotion,' and give the stylist a new title in regards to career level (designer, master stylist, artistic director, and the like). Others simply word it as a 'soft price increase.' It's a good idea to have the price increase info out in the open—either on your station, or at the front desk—so that your client will not be surprised when they go to pay for their services. Never spring a price increase on your client the day of their service. Informing them that there will be a price adjustment upon their next visit—whether that's verbally, displayed conspicuously, posted on your salon website or social media page, or ideally all of the above—shows respect and honesty, two important business values. In my experience, when given notice, clients are willing to support your new pricing. They understand, and you'll be surprised how many congratulate you and support you on your career advancement.

A new issue within the salon industry is gender pricing and discrimination. There are people who believe men and women should be charged the same for their salon services, which contradicts entirely the time equals money theory. What we charge is entirely based on the amount of time it takes us to perform the service properly, as well as the cost of the products used. Typically, from start to finish, women's haircuts take significantly more time than men's. From shampoo time, to blow dry and finish, a woman's service often requires double the amount of time. Women with short hair require more time due to texturing, fringe, etc... and even when men wear longer hair we most often do not flat iron or curl it, or blow it out with a round brush and hairspray, etc. If you find you're conflicted in regards to gender pricing, by all means set a flat rate for every haircut. (If you live in New York City, know many salons have recently received fines due to their gender pricing.) The only way to avoid any conflict in regards to gender pricing and sexual discrimination is to charge by the minute, which could be done in fifteen-minute increments. Then every client would be charged a different price, much like a cab ride. I can't imagine a timer being set, find the notion extremely unprofessional, but it could be a solution I suppose. As a stylist, and equal rights supporter, I believe accusing salons of discrimination because of gender pricing is absurd. Time equals money, as well as attention to detail, experience, and the value you place on your time. That's all. It doesn't need to be so complicated.

Another not so new issue (but equally frustrating) is pricing children's haircuts. Unless you only cater to children, in which case let's assume you've chosen a kids' only hair salon or family style chain, pricing and servicing children in the salon can be dreadful. But it doesn't have to be.

Ironically, gender pricing isn't an issue with kid's haircuts. Salons typically charge anyone under a certain age (usually age 12) the same price. Is it only a matter of time before someone cries foul on this being age discrimination? I doubt it, since children's haircuts are priced lower than adults'. But they often require the same amount of time. Hmm. What to do? Well, if you have a choice, I'd be hesitant to quote a children's haircut price until you knew the head of hair you were going to be dealing with, and could assess how much time they were going to take. Time equals money, remember? Many young girls have just as much hair as their mothers and require just as much time. In addition, many kids will ask if you can curl their hair for them because they're excited to have their hair done and they want to leave feeling extra glamorous, which is understandable and pretty cool actually. A ten-year-old girl takes considerably more time than a ten-year-old boy. Very young children take considerably more time and patience and skill because you're often dealing with a moving canvas, and it's difficult to get a good haircut on a wiggling three-year-old, or a crying, terrified two-year-old. Then there will be those times when you have the honor of giving a baby their first haircut. They might be scared and wiggly, they might be perfectly still, but most infants have such little hair it takes all of five minutes to straighten out the back and cut a few rogue wispy hairs that tend to sprout randomly from a baby's head. So how do you price for the differences here? You can charge a flat rate, and then add on extra services if necessary (for those times the preteen daughter wants a full blow-out or flatiron). Explain first to the parent paying before changing cost because no one likes that kind of surprise at the end of a service. State very clearly your children's cuts include a shampoo and basic blow-dry, and any additional styling services will increase the price. Let this be known before any work has begun to avoid an awkward conversation. You'll have more kids' haircuts in the beginning of your career, because you're available, and your prices are lower. As your book fills and you jump to the next level professionally and your prices reflect that growth you'll have fewer kids on your book. The ones you do have at that point will typically be your established clients' children, and you'll find you'll develop a rapport with the kids as well, which can be refreshing and fun. Watching a child grow and change through the years, and being their hairdresser along the way, is a pretty neat experience.

Price your services accordingly, and don't be afraid to raise your prices as necessary. You'll know (or your employer may suggest) when the time is right. You deserve a raise, just like everyone else. Just be mindful that the quality of your clients' time with you continues to improve as your prices increase. For the time equals money and money equals energy theory goes both ways.

9
PROFESSIONALISM IN THE MODERN SALON

Or, "You Stay Classy, San Diego." *(Anchorman, The Legend of Ron Burgundy)*

"A customer is the most important visitor on our premises; he is not dependent on us. We are dependent on him. He is not an interruption in our work. He is the purpose of it. He is not an outsider in our business. He is part of it. We are not doing him a favor by serving him. He is doing us a favor by giving us an opportunity to do so."
~Mahatma Gandhi

I remember my first experiences in a hair salon well, and if I close my eyes and focus, I can relive those early salon memories. At the time, I lived in a tiny rural town outside of

Louisville, Kentucky. Sometimes we went to the little chain salon in Louisville. (Supercuts or the like.) Honestly, I didn't get my hair cut too often—we couldn't afford it. Our mother usually cut my bangs. But once a year I went to the fancy salon for my back to school perm. The fancy salon, mind you, was either one of two places. In the little town in Kentucky, the local hairdresser ran a salon within her home. She lived upstairs and her salon was on the bottom floor. This is where my grandmother went for her perms and such too. The other fancy salon I knew was located within a department store in the little town my father and stepmother lived in West Virginia. This was during the early eighties and those were my two options.

Back then, you could smoke anywhere. Think Steel Magnolias meets the local smoke-filled tavern. Ashtrays were as common in the salon as gossip magazines. That's what I remember the most—the sight of my too tight perm (look up Richard Simmons, I believe he was my stylist's inspiration) and the smoky smell of my hair. Believe it or not, both the kinky perm and the smell associated with those days are happy memories for me, because I loved going to the salon. I remember sitting beneath the dryer, feeling fancy, observing the ladies talking as they smoked and had their hair done. (I cannot remember a single man being in any salon I went to as a child. I think that is due to both the rural environment both salons were located in, and the fact that the men had their own smoke-filled gossip hub, aka the barber shop.) I sometimes could not believe what I was hearing. Remember, I lived in a small town. Most of the grown-ups knew each other, and most of the school kids did too. The gossip I overheard entertained and sometimes even shocked me.

Fast forward thirty years or so, and it's nearly impossible to imagine this scenario. Times have significantly changed and in our industry they've changed for the better. There's a certain level of professionalism that our clientele expects, and it's in our best interest to exceed their expectations.

Not to mention most of us would be taken aback if we saw a stylist chain smoking while giving an eight-year-old a kinky spiral perm. I, for one, would probably fall over in shock... once the nostalgia wore off.

These days most salons cater equally to men and women, and most successful salons demand a certain degree of professionalism from their stylists. Lack of professionalism is the number one complaint I heard time and time again from salon owners and frustrated stylists. Many of the complaints about our profession that clients shared with me were directly related to lack of professionalism as well. So, it's necessary to examine this.

Professionalism is defined as "the skill, good judgment, and polite behavior that is expected from a person who is trained to do a job well." (Merriam-Webster) It distinguishes you from the amateurs. We are fortunate that salons are regarded as fun and relaxing destinations, so the level of professionalism is not the same as say, a courtroom or doctor's office (thankfully so). That environment would stifle anyone's creativity. But that does not mean we have carte blanche to act like twelve-year-olds. Our clients deserve the utmost respect, as do we. If you want respect, you must give it. If you want to be treated as a professional, not an amateur, you must possess a professional demeanor.

For starters, don't be late. You must put your customers first, and a big part of that means showing up on time. Don't be late to work, and don't leave your clients waiting. I've heard horror stories of clients waiting for close to an hour for their stylist. (I've personally experienced this scenario as a client myself.) This is completely unacceptable. If something arises and you know you are going to be running behind, you owe it to yourself and your clients to explain the situation and give them the option to come back later or re-book. If your day is not going as planned (and trust me, many will) ask the front desk to call your appointments ahead of time, so your clients know what to expect and can plan accordingly. Nothing says "I do not value your time" like running late does. Consider how you feel when a client is late. Even five minutes can make or break your day. Any time I found myself running behind, I made certain the client was notified, either by the front desk or by me personally. People generally respond kindly to calmness and honesty. I'd simply explain that my appointment was taking longer than planned, how sorry I was to keep them waiting, and that just as I would not rush through my current client, I would not rush through them. I'd give them an estimate of when I'd be ready, and offer them a drink and a magazine—anything to make them more comfortable. That is how you handle running behind professionally. What you don't do is ignore their presence, act frazzled and distressed, assume they have nothing else to do, and badmouth anyone involved in your predicament. That is very unprofessional.

Modern technology is amazing, and it works well when for stylists when utilized in a professional manner at work. The tools we have now to make our job easier and more efficient simply did not exist years ago. One of the greatest tools for our industry is the smartphone. With it, we can book appointments, send text reminders, manage our business related social media accounts, and scroll through photos of hairstyles with our clients. At work, this is what our smart phones are for. Anything else is tacky and very unprofessional. So, seriously, when you're working with a client, put your phone away. Texting, chatting, Facebooking... none of it should be done when you have a client in your chair. Your focus and attention should be 100% on them and their hair. Again, think about how you feel when a client is on their phone while you are working on their hair. First of all, it makes our job impossible because their head is cocked sideways, and second of all it's rude. We can't ask them questions freely and don't have their full attention, making communication rough. So, don't be that guy. Unless you're booking their next appointment, taking a photo for your social media page, or swiping their credit card at the end of their service, put your phone away. Use your phone for personal matters whenever you have a break.

As a professional, you should speak highly of others (especially those you work with, and people you admire professionally) and avoid gossip. Gossip is a disease. Don't talk about your personal problems, other stylists, your boss, your mother-in-law, your clients, politics, religion, sex... let your clients talk about such things if they must but don't join in. Talking is natural. Gossiping is not. Keep the conversation on your end focused on your client and hair. If you divulge too much of your personal life, or gossip about others, you risk one or the other coming back and affecting your business negatively. And, of course, it's really unprofessional. Even in the salon.

Be clear on the cost of your services, and always meet or exceed your clients' expectations. If what you and your client decide to do costs more than they are used to, let them know before you begin. Have clear set prices and abide by them. Never assume your clients have the extra money or don't care about a few dollars here or there. Any time a service adds cost to their bill, tell them up front.

Keep your station spotless. It takes maybe one minute to clean your station between clients, so do it. Every time. No one wants to walk on someone else's hair, or see an obviously used comb or brush picked up and placed in their hair. Wipe your chair down, throw your towels in the hamper, put implements away properly, and clear away your used color bowls and brushes. Every client has the right to be seated and served in a fresh work space. Respect your clients and your work space.

Greet each client personally. Eye contact always and a handshake, especially if it's their first time visiting. Some clients want to give you a hug because they love you so much, and vice versa, and that's great too. A warm greeting, a genuine hello, and an authentic desire to please them shines through and shows professionalism. It's also important to walk your clients up the front desk when their service is over. Thank them again, suggest they pre-book, shake their hand or hug them, whatever feels right. Just as we were taught as children, please and thank you go a long way. It's all about being a good person—being grateful for your clients. Showing proper etiquette and having good manners will never go out of fashion.

Anytime a client is unhappy, respond professionally. Although we hate the thought of any unhappy client, it can and does happen, and here you must maintain a high level of professionalism always. Stay calm and composed. Address any concerns before they leave your chair if possible. Do not be arrogant or argumentative. If you happen to receive a negative review online, again, be very professional in responding. It's best if any issues are addressed in person, but these days some people go straight to Yelp or the like to vent their frustrations, allowing potentially millions of people to read the negative review. Let those people see your positive reply and professionalism. The Internet is a huge gift to our industry when utilized properly. Ideally you won't receive any negative reviews online, but if you do, take a deep breath and respond professionally.

Communicate, communicate, communicate. It's your responsibility to ask the right questions, to be an expert in your field, and then to deliver on the promises you make. The majority of hairstyling mishaps are a result of poor communication. A true professional also helps others in need. If you sense a co-worker is struggling with a client—having a hard time communicating or choosing the right color formula, etc... reach out to your co-worker discreetly—let them know you're there to help out if they're in a bind. Two heads are better than one, and every person brings value to the salon, so share your knowledge and don't be afraid or too ego-centered to ask others for help when necessary.

The number one rule (of course) is the golden rule. Treat others how you expect to be treated. Put yourself in the client's shoes and imagine how they feel when they come in to see you. Imagine how you'd like them to feel when they walk out the door, and then act accordingly.

10
OH, THAT'S PERSONAL
Aligning Your Personality With Your Image

"Personality has power to uplift, power to depress, power to curse, and power to bless."
~ Paul Harris

One of the greatest joys of being a hairdresser is talking to people all day long—sharing your gifts and talent with them, listening to their unique experiences and perspectives. We are part of an elite few who get paid to have fun, can make people feel good, and are free to chat openly and laugh loudly in the work environment. Being a hairstylist is very cool. We also get to see the fruits of our labor immediately. Nothing is more satisfying than seeing a smile on your client's face, as you both enjoy the finished product that you created.

It's amazing what stylists get to do, hear, and experience

each day. Our clients tell us *everything*. You hear all kinds of stories when you're a hairstylist. Some will make you laugh until you cry; some will break your heart. Others will annoy you. Sometimes we have to bite our tongue; sometimes we are sought after for personal advice. We are the highest-paid social workers and the lowest-paid therapists.

Once you've established good hair rapport, a relationship forms and there's no limit or rules to what your clients can and will discuss with you. I will not divulge anything personal a client has shared with me—and you never should as well. What I want to discuss is what I've shared about myself with clients.

Almost nothing.

How can that be, you ask? When I say nothing I don't mean it literally—but do I talk to my clients about personal issues I'm trying to resolve? No. Do they know if I'm having problems in my private life? Do they know about struggles I may be having with a family member? Do they know I'm broke because last week I was sick and I may or may not make a profit and be able to cover my loft rent and supplies? Do I ask them for advice on any of my personal matters?

No. No. No. And no.

Here's why. At one of the salons I worked for, a new client called in searching for a stylist. Our receptionist asked her a bit about her hair—was it short, long, color treated, straight, curly, etc. Our receptionist asked these questions so that she could place the new client with just the right stylist. The woman replied, "I'm not concerned about any of that—just please give me someone who doesn't complain about their life." It turns out she was new to the city, and had experienced a series of disappointing salon visits. Was she disappointed about her hair? Nope. She was burnt out from listening to stylists who complained about their personal lives while they were doing her hair. So, while we're expected to listen to our clients, we cannot turn the situation around and unload on them. Your clients are there to relax and unwind, not to carry your burdens home with them.

Consider the following testimony, shared with me by a female client in her twenties, describing her first visit to a stylist and how poorly it went:

"The first time I head into a new salon to see a new stylist I feel anxious and overwhelmed. It's nerve-wracking to have to sit with a total stranger for such a long period of time (two hours usually in my case because I get highlights and a haircut). I'm a girl who doesn't feel comfortable with silence, so I worry what if we don't have anything to talk about? It's scary! Or worse, what if he / she has too much to say and I begin to glaze over and zone out and forget to respond, like I often do when people talk too much! I say this because I once had a stylist who had too much to say about her family, friends, community, politics... And it wasn't just stories or funny stuff—it was her venting and pushing her opinions on me and looking for me to team up with her against the world! I just wanted to chat and get my hair

done! I never went back to that salon, even though my hair turned out fine. She was just too creepy and overbearing. A stylist should be educated on how much you should tell someone you barely know. There's a lot to consider when you have different personalities coming in and out of your chair all day long."

You could be the best hairdresser in the world, but if you don't know when to keep things private, and you're constantly complaining, you will have a very difficult time building and maintaining a clientele. And those clients who do stay with you will be complainers as well—like attracts like. Positive people attract positive people. Negative people attract negative people. And negative people are harder to get away from. We all know that feeling—don't make your chair a space for negativity.

Some days, it will seem as if you are every client's therapist, and you will find yourself emotionally exhausted by the end of the day. People tend to share so much of themselves with their stylist. You may feel inclined to share equally with them, to unload some of your stresses and uncertainties, but you can't. Clients want to unwind. They want to relax. They want to leave the salon lighter, in every way. I promise you this—even if they ask you personal questions, they really don't want to hear overly detailed answers. Even if they tell you intimate details about their life, they don't want to hear every intimate detail of yours.

Take a step back and imagine being the client of someone who complains too much. How would you feel if you got together with a friend once a month or so, and all they did was complain about their life? And on top of that, imagine paying to hear them complain. This rule is often difficult to follow, for many of our clients become our friends. But friend or not, if you're exchanging money for a service— they are your clients and you are their stylist. They are paying you to feel good and look good. You are not paying them for a therapy session. It's okay if they tell you personal details you'd rather not hear. This rule only goes one way. They do care for you, but salon time is their relaxation time. Don't ruin it unintentionally.

If your personal life is not going the way you want it to, or if you're having personal issues that are difficult to resolve, of course you're going to want and need to talk about them. If you're unable to discuss such matters with your family or a close friend, seek your own therapist to work them out. Make the time to work on you privately, so that you can focus on your clients and career while at the salon. Your needs are important. Personal problems and unresolved issues demand to be addressed, just not with your clients, or in your place of business. Not to mention, when you focus day in and day out on the negativity in your life, and talk about it at length with your clientele or co-workers, you're delaying the act of finding a solution to the issues you may be facing, and you are attracting more negativity. While at the salon, be mindful of where you're putting your energy. When you're not at the salon, work just as hard at having healthy and meaningful relationships, and seek advice when you need to.

What we say sets the tone of our work environment. It distinguishes us as professionals. When we speak poorly of ourselves, complain about our life, speak poorly of another stylist or salon, it sends the message that gossip and negativity are welcomed and encouraged near you, leaving little room or energy for positivity. When you're at the salon, you should focus on your client, their hair, the 'now,' and how to make your business flourish. And remember, your personality—your creativity, your artistic gift, your love of people—is part of what brought you to hair design in the first place. Never lose that creative, fun, artistic person by burying him or her in a sea of mindless negative chatter. Especially at work, where you're allowed to create and be free. The salon can be your happy place, your little refuge too, if you let it be.

While we're on the subject of personal, let's take a moment to discuss personal grooming and self-expression.

The hair salon is one work environment where you are expected and encouraged to express yourself artistically, both in the hairstyles you create, the way you wear your own hair, and in the way you choose to dress. We have the freedom to dress and adorn our bodies to our liking. How can we inspire others to express their true selves if we are repressed? Granted, some salons and spas have dress codes, and at times they are necessary if the salon or spa has a specific vibe they are trying to achieve. You, as a stylist, will determine if that kind of work environment is right for you. The first salon I worked with did in fact have a dress code. We could only wear black or white. Considering

I typically only wore black at the time I didn't mind at all. (In fact, many hairdressers choose to wear all black regardless. Black clothing easily hides color stains.) As a whole we did look professional and consistent. The all-black attire helped to distinguish the salon professionals from the clientele. We appeared polished, united, and it suited the high-end salon atmosphere.

I also once worked (briefly) as an assistant in a salon that, although it did not have a specific dress code, had strict rules regarding various forms of self expression. Visible tattoos were not allowed. Hair had to be a natural color—no blues, pinks, 'punk' colors of any form. I believe if you have tattoos and prefer not to worry if they are visible or not you shouldn't have to. If you love boldly colored hair and it looks good on you, you should wear it. One of the greatest things about being a hairstylist is you can be yourself, and as long as you're good at what you do, your clients will love you and follow you—regardless of any tattoo, piercing, or avant-garde style. Many clients I speak with appreciate their stylist's unique style. They wish they worked in an environment that welcomed and encouraged self-expression. Many people are afraid to get a tattoo or a piercing or to push the envelope with their hair color. Regardless if they ever take the plunge, they appreciate a stylist who is authentic. Hair is art. Hair salons are art galleries. Freedom of expression is a beautiful thing.

There are of course people who do prefer their stylists to be more on the conservative side. There are salons and stylists out there for them. And of course there are stylists who are most comfortable working in a conservative environment. Therein lies the beauty of this business—you can't throw a glance and not see a hair salon, remember? And each salon is as diverse and unique as the people that walk through their doors.

Be yourself. There's a salon out there just right for you.

Another important reason to express yourself confidently is your clientele will begin to mirror you. Your clients will, for the most part, have a personality similar to yours, because again—like attracts like. It happens naturally. This is a profession where your personality is allowed to shine. Regardless if you're in a high-end salon with a dress code or a small space with no rules whatsoever, if you do your job well, are a professional, and let people know you truly care, your clients will find you, stay with you, and love you for who you are.

While it's important to feel comfortable in your own skin, so that you can create organically, it is equally important to be impeccable with your personal grooming. Remember—we get very close to people. Your clients can smell where you've been the night before. They know if you've had too much coffee or too many cigarettes. They see the mascara from last night. Everyone knows when you're hung-over. Our armpits are in their noses. Our breath is in their face. You can't hide your sins and bad habits. Your teeth, your perfume, your lunch—all of it is apparent.

Reputable salon owners will not hire a disheveled stylist.

I've witnessed stylists with plenty of potential get turned away simply because they had horrible breath and that was all the salon owner could focus on. It seems so simple, yet this must be addressed.

Your appearance and grooming habits tell the world where you are personally and professionally. We are in the business of beauty. So, dress how you feel best. Decorate your body how you see fit. Wear your hair any way you wish. Be there for your clients to talk to, and remember not to use them as your therapist. Above all, take care of yourself, so that you are ready and equipped to take care of others.

11
INTERVIEW: ROBERT HENSCHEL
Hairstylist Extraordinaire Since 1964

"Choose a job you love, and you will never have to work a day in your life."
~ Confucius

As fate would have it, my father-in-law is a hairdresser too. Rob has been a hairstylist for fifty years, and shows no sign of stopping. He has no plans of retiring soon, because he feels like when he goes to work he "gets to play." Why would he want to quit playing every day?

I pinned Rob down one evening after work—at sixty-nine years strong, he's still putting in kick-ass days at the salon.

So, Rob, what it is you enjoy the most about being a hairstylist?

The creativity and the contact with people.

What surprised you the most about the business when you began working in a salon?

The length of time it took to develop my business. I was surprised by the amount of patience it took.

On that note, what advice do you have for someone just entering the business?

Be patient. That's the biggie, because it doesn't happen overnight. You have to be patient in many ways. And, it's patience with people... the client base, you know, because no matter what, they're the ones that are paying you. You're not doing them a favor. They're paying you for your expertise. That's my advice. Be patient. And, just know how to be nice... even if it's the hardest thing in the world to do. Be nice.

I've written a bit about keeping your personal life separate from work, which is hard sometimes because obviously we talk to people all day long, and a sort of friendship is formed with your clientele. Any advice or thoughts on that subject?

My rule of thumb has always been if the client asks you something, then they want to hear the story. But if you're having trouble in life, don't bore the client with it. And the other advice I always give somebody that's new to the business is—when you get to the door, no matter how bad you feel, whether you have a hangover... I don't care what it is... turn it off and smile. Force it. Smile. Let them think that you're happy as can be. Because it's important. If they pick up bad vibes from you, you won't keep that person.

You know, I have a client, she's now seventy-seven years old, and she's the very first person, the very first head of hair, that I ever touched.

Really? She still comes to you?

Fifty years later I still have her.

Why do you think that is?

I think, well, I think I'm like a friend. And basically, I think it has to do with listening. That's a lot of it, is listening. Then you develop camaraderie with your clients. They're not 'social friends' per se, but when they sit down in your chair, you're their confidant. You're there for them.

You point out that your clients aren't social friends...

You really shouldn't cross that line. I mean, there are a couple over the years I've hung out with socially... you'll run into your clients outside of the salon, and that's great, but yeah, you have to keep that separate.

Can you think of any 'cons' to being a hairstylist? Some of the aspects that aren't so great?

Things that are not so great... hmm... well the only thing I can think of is everybody thinks it's just a piece of cake, and it is hard. It's also hard on your body. It takes its toll. Your legs, your back, your shoulders... basically that's the only thing I can think of. I am so passionate, and that's another thing that is so important—if you don't have a passion for what you're doing, forget it, because you won't last. I read a statistic regarding the amount of stylists who quit within one year. It's staggering. You have to have that passion. There again, I think they think "I'm going to go to the salon, I'm going to make a million bucks a week," and you know what, it doesn't happen that way. It took me seven years to build my business before I could say that I truly felt comfortable.

Have you ever owned your own salon?

Yes. For twenty-eight years. In fact, I owned the salon I work in now.

As a salon owner, what were some things that would frustrate you about the other stylists—the ones working for you?

Attitude. There were some who felt they were doing the client a favor, instead of recognizing the client was the one doing you a favor sitting in your chair. I had to preach that more than anything.

If given the opportunity to do it all over again, would you still choose to be a salon owner?

Absolutely. It was extremely rewarding for me, and fit my personality.

You mentioned you work at the salon you once owned. At this stage of your career, how does it feel to go to work each day?

Well, I play there. (wink) But yes, now I booth rent from the person I sold my salon to. I've been there for forty-one years. And at this stage in my life, I literally feel like I go and play every day.

Any advice on how to save for retirement? For many salons, the idea of a 401k or savings plan is non-existent.

Your retirement's on your own. You have to learn how to manage your money. This is where a lot of people screw up. When it comes time, the money's gotta be there.

You know, for those who are extremely artistic, and who aren't interested in managing the business side of things, this is where I see a lot of stylists get in over their head. They go into a booth rental situation, because they can make more money, and be their own boss—come and go as they want to—but they may not be business people... so they end up owing the government taxes, they don't know how to put aside money, and you gotta have that. If you're not the type of person who can manage these things, you're better off staying in a commission salon, so that you don't even have to think about it. Let someone else run the business side for you. At least your taxes and social security are withdrawn for you. You're not going to make as much money, but you will have more freedom, less worry.

Is there an amount or percentage you recommend stylists

set aside each pay period towards their retirement savings?

You can't really do that, because each week is different, and when I had little kids I put away almost nothing because we chose to live on one income—mine, and there was simply not enough to really save. Some weeks if I put ten bucks a week aside, that was plenty. But the key is I never stopped. I've always put something away into an investment. Now I can afford to put away a good amount. The men in my family live a long time. I plan to live until at least ninety.

So, you've been doing hair for fifty years. When did you know you were going to be a hairdresser?

When I was a kid I was always enamored with hair when I would go to the barber shop. So, my first thoughts were that I'd be a barber. Well then things changed, and I became more interested in being a hairdresser because I liked being around beautiful women, so... why should I be a barber? (laughs) And that actually is when I decided what I was going to do.

How would you say the business has changed the most in the past fifty years?

Oh my god... well first of all the biggest change is the technology. You have to remember, when I started in the business in 1964...

.... let me just say that's so awesome. You got to do hair in the seventies and eighties, which must have been

amazing….

You got it. But when I started, there weren't even rollers. We used fingerwaves and pincurls. There were no tools like we have now. So much has changed. Products, the improvements in color… I've been through it all, through all the stages from the big bouffant to the angel curl things, oh god… prom time… to today—precise cutting, blowing it dry, letting it go…

…color is wonderful now.

You know, as a stylist, you always watch trends, which I've always felt is important… but lots of hairdressers learn the "latest thing" and then put it on everybody. Which is awful. That's not creativity. Style should depend on the hair and the person, and a lot of trends aren't attractive on certain people. Hair quality, hair texture, face shape… that's more important than any trend. And you have to develop confidence in yourself to listen to what the client wants, yet have the nerve to say "you know what, with your hair texture and face shape, would you be open to…" and then suggest what will look best. Also, show your clients how to do their hair. They're not hairstylists. You must show them how to do their hair. You know, we can do anything to the hair, but can they do it?

Thank you so much for talking with me. Any final words of advice?

If you're loyal to your client, they will be loyal back. Have self confidence but not arrogance. Always act professional

—none of this silly small-talk.

Remember it's all about what you do. If you take good care of that client, if you relate to the client... they will tell ten other people about you. It's all about word-of-mouth.

And never think that you've learned it all.

12
FIRST IMPRESSIONS
The Art of Shampooing

"Nothing is so healing as the human touch."
~ Bobby Fischer

As hairstylists, we touch people all day. It's part of our job, and this gift of touch is unique to our industry. Clients often walk into the salon after a long day at work or an afternoon with their children. It's their escape from the ordinary. Very few float in, already relaxed.

Many of you may be wondering why I'm dedicating an entire chapter to shampooing. The way you shampoo a client's hair can take their salon experience from great to heavenly; from fantastic to divine. The time and attention you give while shampooing your clients is just as important as a proper consultation, for communication also take place in the way you give a shampoo. Taking the time to really care for your client and their well-being lets them know they literally are in good hands with you.

When asked how they feel about their time spent at the salon, many clients told me the shampoo is the best part of their day. They believe a good scalp massage makes "all the difference," and one gentleman even went so far as to say it was "the third best feeling in life; second is a hug, and the first is obvious."

No other occupation, besides nursing, gives you the opportunity to shampoo someone else's hair. Think about that for a minute. Stop and remember the last time someone else shampooed your hair for you. More importantly, think about the way in which they did so. It's a feeling you can't get anywhere else. A friend of mine shared a sweet memory with me in regards to why she enjoys the shampoo so much. She said, "I almost feel like a child again, having my mama wash my hair. If it's quiet, and done thoughtfully and tenderly, it can be truly therapeutic."

You and your client have an opportunity to bond over this part of the service. You can watch your client relax and surrender. The effects of a proper head massage are as healing and rejuvenating as a full body massage. Do not have a conversation with them at this time. Let them melt. You have hopefully already had a consultation with them, and you will continue to talk once you're back at your chair. We all lead hectic, busy lives. The shampoo bowl is a time for them to simply relax and feel peaceful. We are exclusively granted permission to touch our clients this way and expect nothing back in return. We, as stylists, may be one of the only people permitted to do so. I take this very seriously. It's a unique component to our industry and should be honored. All humans deserve a kind gesture (here via a thoughtful shampoo).

To give a proper shampoo, you need to slow down during the process, and never rush. I know you're busy and have a schedule to stick with. Keep in mind, a relaxing, therapeutic shampoo is a simple gift we can give our clients. It doesn't have to take forever; it just needs to be done with intention. There is a fine line between 'relaxing' and 'too much.' You can give a calming shampoo in under five minutes. Leave enough room with your appointment scheduling to do so.

Why? For one, while shampooing your client you have the opportunity to provide an immediate feeling of well-being and stress relief. Many of us hold stress and tension in our neck and scalp. It also benefits your business by opening the lines of communication further, for a relaxed client is an open client. They are more inclined to talk freely and more candidly about what they'd like to achieve with their hairstyle. They're also more apt to listen to your suggestions once relaxed. They feel content and connected to you when they sit back in your styling chair. They will be more authentic, and you will be as well. When authentic dialogue exchanges, everyone's happy and satisfied. Both you and your client deserve this type of exchange. This also increases the probability of your client returning to you, and referring additional friends and family to you, therefore building your business. Clients believe that a great shampoo is the prelude to a great haircut. When asked, many clients also replied that they base the amount of tip they give their stylists largely on the shampoo or massage. In fact, my husband commented that before I began cutting his hair, even if he didn't like the haircut he'd received from someone, he would always tip well if they gave him a relaxing shampoo.

It's important to point out there are a few things clients do not like during this part of their service. Many mentioned they prefer the conversation to stop so they can completely relax. Others expressed irritation if they felt the products weren't rinsed thoroughly—if they were left feeling shampoo or conditioner on their neck or behind their ears. (People with thick hair mentioned this annoyance most often.) And no one can relax if their head and neck feel sore from improper positioning in the shampoo sink. Always make sure their neck is comfortable, and place a towel or some form of cushioning if need be to soften the point of contact.

Hone your skills at the shampoo bowl. Pay attention when your hair is being washed by someone else, and take note as to what feels good, and what doesn't. Practice giving your coworkers and friends a scalp massage, and ask for feedback. It's amazing what a genuine act of kindness—a simple shampoo—can do for your clients and for you. There's no easier or kinder way to build your business.

13
A GOOD HAIRDRESSER IS HARD TO FIND
Putting Yourself in the Client's Chair

"The customer's perception is your reality."
~Kate Zabriskie

We've previously discussed professionalism in the workplace, one of the most important factors to becoming a successful stylist. Now we'll discuss one of the secrets to giving your clients the best salon experience possible—by frequently being a client yourself. One of the best ways to understand how your clients feel is to put yourself in another stylist's chair. It's a great way for you to recognize first-hand what it is you do and don't want your clients to experience when they are with you.

If you're brave, you'll go incognito—to a salon where no

one knows you, to a stylist you've never seen before. It's what our clients do when they come to us for the first time, yet just the thought of such role reversal makes most stylists cringe. What if you hate your hair? What if they mess up the color? What if you don't get along with the stylist?

These are the exact same thoughts every new client experiences when they go to a new stylist. Including you.

You can learn a lot from experiencing other stylists' techniques—their talent and their shortcomings. When you experience someone's great or poor customer service style, it serves to remind you how important good customer service is and how you want your clients to be treated. I'll let you know, it's hard to be a client once you've been doing hair for quite some time. But it's important to put your hair in someone else's hands so you can remember what it's like to be in the chair. It's a vulnerable place. Never forget that.

Hopefully, when you go to the salon you leave loving your hair. But what if you don't? Imagine for a moment you hate your haircut. Imagine it's not at all what you envisioned; too short, too long, or worse—too long in some spots and too short in others. You cannot style it or hide it or pull it back. Perhaps to everyone else, it doesn't "look so bad" but for you, in your mind and your emotional state, you believe it is the worst haircut you've ever had. In short, imagine being a client terribly disappointed with your salon experience.

Sounds terrible, right? And near impossible for a hairstylist to imagine. We're lucky. We usually know the person cutting our hair. We talk the lingo. We micro-manage our haircuts. We're fortunate to rarely, if ever, receive a bad haircut.

Our clients aren't so lucky. Often they come into our life scarred from a previous haircut experience such as the one I asked you to imagine before. Sometimes we—yes, you and I—are responsible for giving a "bad" haircut. This is why I think it's important to step out of your comfort zone and be someone's new client from time to time. It's a learning experience you simply cannot duplicate any other way.

A few years ago I sat down in the chair to have my hair cut. I had been growing out a bob with the intention of wearing longer hair. I explained to the stylist that I needed a little trim but wanted to keep the length. I was leaving for vacation the next day and wanted to still be able to pull my hair back while on the beach. He appeared to listen, and then proceeded to cut four inches off the back of my hair. When I felt the first snip, I was in shock. Did it look terrible? No. And it wasn't technically a bad haircut. But it was not what I wanted. At all. I had very few styling options. It drove me nuts. It was not what I envisioned, and that's what made it an upsetting experience for me. Being a hairstylist, I was able to better cope, thinking *it's only hair, it'll grow...* I could roll with it. I could style it. That haircut was over three years ago.

And guess what? I haven't forgotten about it, now have I?

I've also had amazing hair experiences, where I've left the salon feeling about as new and beautiful as a woman can feel; where I couldn't help but smile, despite driving home in rush hour traffic. These experiences I remember, and crave, but they're never 100% guaranteed when I'm playing 'client.' Like everyone else, I'm always nervous, yet ever-hopeful.

Unfortunately, bad experiences tend to linger longer in one's memory. A few months after giving birth to my second son, I decided to visit book an appointment at a salon near my house, so I could relax instead of squeezing in a quick haircut at work between clients. I arrived on time, saw that the hairdresser I was scheduled with was blow-drying someone's hair, signaling to me that he was almost ready. I grabbed a coffee, a magazine, and waited for my turn. Then I watched him shampoo someone else with color on her hair, and then begin cutting her hair. A half hour later, I was still waiting. And furious. Clients scheduled after me were trickling in, waiting beside me in the waiting room, stifling their annoyance as well. I got up and left. For some reason I apologized when I explained that I only had a small window of time due to the fact I was breastfeeding and needed to get home and couldn't wait any longer for my appointment. The stylist laughed and said, "You know how crazy things can get" and asked if I could come back tomorrow morning. I wanted to say, "No, I can't. I have a job and two children and I booked a haircut for today, not tomorrow...and by the way I'm a hairstylist too." But instead I said I'd call soon and then—get this—for some reason I told him to have a nice evening. I was so disappointed. I just wanted to relax and have someone wash my hair and give me a new look. I couldn't believe that this was a stylist in a high end salon charging $65 a haircut, and yet he was so unprofessional. How utterly embarrassing for our industry. Are clients' expectations so low, or do certain stylists take their clients so for granted that waiting close to an hour is the norm? I had a renewed respect for myself, for the salon I worked in, and a new sense of confidence knowing I would never run my business in such a manner.

That experience was over ten years ago... and yep, I still remember it vividly.

This is how we hope (and therefore we must make it our goal) that a client of ours never feels.

Both my good and my bad hair memories have all been teaching moments for me. They put me on the opposite side of the chair, and for that I'm grateful. I challenge you to be a client every once in awhile, to go somewhere new; to be vulnerable and nervous, in order to remember exactly how it feels.

14
SOCIAL MEDIA
Building Your Business Online

"The more you engage with customers the clearer things become and the easier it is to determine what you should be doing."
~ John Russell

Hair salons are social work places, so it only makes sense that social media act as an extension of the salon—a way to continue to share the happenings going on, both with you and your salon business. Social media can be an extremely useful tool for any hairstylist. It's free, easy to utilize, and its potential to reach and influence your clientele should not be underestimated. Social media is word-of-mouth, and word-of-mouth is the best way to build a solid, lasting client base.

There are many social media platforms from which to choose. I recommend selecting one or two social media sites to promote your business, so you can focus your energy and not feel overwhelmed. Of course, if multi-tasking is your thing, go for it and promote yourself on as many platforms as you'd like. Regardless, it's important to choose the platforms that feel right and come naturally to you.

For example, if you're already familiar with Facebook (and really, who isn't?) creating a separate Facebook page for your salon business is easy and fairly effortless. With over 500 million people on Facebook, odds are many of your clients already use the social media site. You should create a separate Facebook page dedicated specifically to your salon business. While many stylists simply 'friend' their clients on their personal Facebook page, I caution against this. Why? First of all, it's more professional to have a separate Facebook page for your business. Second, you can keep your life outside of work private, something I feel is important long term. It's easy to get a Facebook page going. Simply create a page then invite your current friends and family to 'like' your page. As you build your clientele, invite your clients to like your page as well. Include your social media pages on your business cards. Some stylists offer a small one-time discount to their clients for liking or following them online. You have the freedom to do what you wish.

If photography is your thing, you should definitely have an Instagram, Pintrest, Tumblr, or Flickr account. One or more of these accounts in addition to Facebook and/or Twitter enables you to cross-promote from one platform to the next. Again, choose wisely. Unless you know you can juggle several social media platforms effortlessly, be selective and dedicate yourself to just one or two. A neglected social media business site is worse than having no web presence at all.

Once your platforms are established, remember to stay active and engaged. The dialogue and branding built online is similar to that which happens in the salon. It should be professional and fun. Engage with your audience. Ask questions, answer their questions, show off your work and let your personality shine. Create your own hashtags. Make your online portfolio as big and as broad as you want it to be. Just like in the salon itself, your online presence and its success will be a direct result of the effort and enthusiasm you put into it.

What type of content should your social media page contain?

Post before and after pics of your clients (of course, only if clients allow. Many will be flattered when you ask permission to post their picture online, and will want to share these pics on their Facebook wall as well). When you tag both your client and your salon in the picture, their friends will be able to see their new style, and there it is... word-of-mouth via social media. The average Facebook user has 130 friends; therefore your name and your work have the potential to reach 130 new people for every picture you post and tag. As you can see, cross-promoting with pictures is essential. Visual testimonies of your work speak for themselves. Having an Instagram or Pintrest picture to cross-promote onto Facebook or Twitter is not only fun, but effective free marketing. Do yourself a favor, and photograph your clients in flattering light, or install a nice filter app on your camera device. People photograph best in soft natural light, and it's details like this that will guarantee every picture you share is a flattering one.

Post articles and photos pertaining to latest hair trends, and information on how you can help your clients achieve the newest looks. Don't be afraid to state your opinion as well. If you believe the latest trend is tacky or unattractive, say so! The last thing you want to do is promise to deliver on a look that you find appalling, or a trend that will be short lived and frowned upon.

Share any news regarding your training and continuing education. Clients love to hear about your commitment to your profession. This adds value to your service, especially during times of price increases. Your enthusiasm is contagious. When you attend a show or take a class and come back bursting with new ideas, it stimulates your clients' enthusiasm as well, and keeps work from becoming dull or routine.

Share pictures or videos of your salon space and of you in action. This is great for Facebook, Instagram, Tumblr,Flickr, Yelp, Pintrest, and Vine. Again, you should cross-promote to your various platforms—not only to reach the highest amount of clientele, but to continually share your creative vision.

Share hairstyling tips and tricks (this can be especially useful and fun). You can even create your own Youtube channel, and film step-by-step videos showing how to create certain looks. If you decide to have a Youtube account, be sure to cross-promote your Youtube page on your Facebook page. (Can I stress this enough?)

Share promotions, specials you may be offering, holiday well wishes, statements of gratitude for your clients and their continued business.

Post reminders to book ahead, especially during busy times of the year,

Post any current or last minute openings you may have that day or week. (I can't tell you how many times I had an appointment cancel and posted the appointment opening on my Facebook page, resulting in that appointment being filled within minutes.)

Do **NOT** post:

Complaints or rants about your day or pet peeves about clients.

Anything controversial (political postings, religious views, etc...) Save that for your personal page if you must.

Do not over sell products or services on your social media sites. An occasional promotion or sales pitch is fine. Too many will offend and become annoying—the exact opposite of your social media goals.

Of course, all this online presence works both ways. What do you do when someone posts a negative comment online regarding you, your salon, or your work? It can be crushing, kill your self esteem, and leave you feeling both hurt and angry. Before responding to any negativity, take a deep breath. Then, be as professional as possible. Hopefully, if a client is unsatisfied, they will approach you first—not go online with a public review. Unfortunately, some do go straight online—that's simply the yin and yang of social media and public websites.

If you get a negative review, it's important to address the reviewer and offer them the opportunity for you to adjust their hairstyle so that they are happy. Resist the urge to engage in any negative banter. You must keep it clean and professional. Explain to them that you wish for them to love their hair, and if they are unhappy to contact you so you can make it right. You can also address the review in a broader sense by making a general mission statement reply—again stressing that your goal is to have your clients leave feeling wonderful. Turn the negative review into an opportunity to show your professional attitude towards your craft, and your desire to please your clientele. Most importantly, use the opportunity to show you care.

Gone are the days when we opened up the phonebook searching for a salon. Most people reach for their smartphones and computers to research a new product, person or company. This is why being actively engaged online is so important. Word-of-mouth will always reign when it comes to gaining new clients, but these days, with technology what it is, word-of-mouth happens in many ways—not just through person-to-person exchange. Someone simply 'liking' your page on Facebook, or sharing your photo on Tumblr, can have a huge impact on getting your name out to the broader community—connecting you to those whom you would not have been able to reach before the days of social media.

15
MAKING MISTAKES
How to Avoid Them and What to Do When You
Make One

"Your most unhappy customers are your
greatest source of learning."
~Bill Gates

I have a friend who believes the two scariest careers a
person can have are stand-up comedian and hairdresser. He
believes there is no room for error or failure with either
career, for the mere thought of telling a joke in front of an
audience that's expecting to laugh, or cutting someone's
hair that is expecting perfection, equally terrifies him.

Messing up. It is our biggest fear. And here's the reality. It's
going to happen. We all make mistakes. Sometimes we go

into a cut or color nervous, other times we realize mid-way through something's not right; sometimes it's not until we begin to blow dry our client's hair we realize (and most likely, your client does too) that something has gone wrong.

Having a color or cut not turn out the way you expect is very distressing—for both you and your client. Sometimes the fault is 100% ours. With color, we may notice at the shampoo bowl that the tone or level of the color we've chosen isn't quite what we desired. Perhaps we chose the wrong developer, failed to take into consideration previous color on the hair or underlying pigments, or simply applied the wrong product onto the hair. (It happens—you're busy and grab the wrong color tube... color was put away in the wrong place, someone else mixed your color for you wrong, etc...) Sometimes miscommunication is to blame, and it's not until the service is complete that we find out our client is disappointed with the end result. Sometimes we assume the color formula in our record books is the correct one, when it could have been recorded there improperly. There are many reasons, but few excuses. And no matter what the reason, a mistake needs to be fixed as soon as possible. It's unethical to allow a client to pay for a job poorly done, or to assume they can live with a look they aren't pleased with.

The hardest part is admitting your mistake.

Mistakes can throw off your entire day—for both emotional and practical reasons. Emotionally they can wreck your self-esteem and confidence. Practically they can create chaos on your book, causing you to run behind schedule—which is also emotionally distressing. They can upset your clients and throw their schedule off as well. Mistakes create a lot of stress but you have to acknowledge when they happen, and make the situation right, ideally before your client leaves your chair.

As Benjamin Franklin said, "An ounce of prevention is worth a pound of cure." Here are a few tips to prevent hair color mistakes from happening:

Use pictures. With today's technology, pulling up examples of hair color via your smart phone or salon computer is easy, common, and expected. If a client hasn't brought in a photograph, you should find one. It's often much easier to show a picture than to try to explain color nuances with words. What red is to one person is entirely different to another. Photos prevent many mistakes from ever happening.

Study your client's skin tone and natural hair color, and know which tones will and will not work with their natural features. Know your limits and do not make promises you cannot fulfill.

Ask for help. In the best salons, stylists work together and co-workers are a team. If you're unsure what route to take, ask for a second opinion from someone you trust. We all have special gifts and bring varied experiences and perspectives to the table. (If you work somewhere that does not encourage teamwork and brainstorming, might I suggest you find a new salon, and soon.) Also, clients enjoy more than one hairdresser consulting with them. It actually makes them feel special and confident in your abilities, so never worry that asking for advice makes you look uneducated. Quite the opposite actually—it shows you're smart enough to gather a second opinion—which is both professional and caring.

It seems so simple, but **verify every single color tube or bottle before you begin mixing.** Make sure level six ash wasn't put where level six gold should be, and so on… Also check your client's current hair status before mixing any formula, even a tried and true formula you've used on them for years. Hair texture and percentage of gray can change suddenly. What once worked will periodically need adjusting.

Often we get so busy we forget to immediately write down adjustments to a client's hair color formula, thinking we will remember it, or get around to documenting the formula later. Try not to let this happen. Minuscule amounts of color can impact the outcome significantly. What's the difference between a twenty-dollar color retouch and a seventy-dollar retouch? Attention to detail, and consistency.

Making a mistake with a haircut is often more difficult to fix than a color mistake. With a haircut, there's no way to undo what's been done, unless the error is you've left the hair too long. Drastic haircut mistakes most often happen while in cosmetology school and at the beginning of your career. They can be due to a lack of training, a lack of experience, improper apprenticeship guidance, over-confidence, and poor communication skills. With haircutting, you cannot undo what's been done.

Here are some tips to avoiding haircut mistakes:

Consult, consult, consult. As with color, photos are very important with haircutting and can aid in deterring any miscommunication. Knowing exactly what you want your end result to look like is essential before you take a single snip.

Take your time. Hair is easy to get lost in. Especially if you're new to the floor, a client with gobs of hair can be very intimidating. In fact, any hair type, when straightened or blown smooth, shows every single scissor line. It is important you take your time cutting all hair types and educate yourself on how to properly cut and blend different hair textures.

Cutting hair properly takes practice. With every haircut you improve. Your skill only improves with time and experience. There's no shortcut to the craft. You are essentiaily taking a visual idea and turning it into something you can touch and feel. Something another human being is going to wear on their body every single day. Some take to it quicker than others. Until you feel confident and develop the visual skills necessary to execute a haircut properly, give yourself plenty of haircutting time. When you're new to cutting hair, I recommend booking your haircuts in hour-long increments, at minimum. It's better to work patiently through a perfect haircut, then to be rushed in the course of a flawed one.

Some salons offer quick trims (where you do not shampoo the hair beforehand or blow it dry) at a lower price. This is a recipe for sub-par haircutting. How anyone can cut unwashed dirty hair properly and with pride, I'll never understand. Your client's service needs to be complete, beginning with a proper shampoo and ending with a beautiful blow-dry. Not to mention, most of the time a great haircut is made even better by the finishing details and fine-tuning we perform after drying the hair. Therefore, I do not believe in cutting hair that hasn't been shampooed. And I don't believe in letting a client leave with wet hair.

What's the difference between a ten-dollar haircut and a hundred-dollar haircut? A twenty-dollar color and a two-hundred-dollar color? The details. What's the best way to avoid mistakes? The details. What's the best way to handle a mistake once made? The details.

So, while making a mistake on your client's hair is certainly no laughing matter... just as some of the best intended jokes often fall flat, so will your best intended hair attempts. And similar to professional comedians, you will sometimes find you have to admit when you've stumbled then go back and make it right. Paying close attention to detail, acknowledging and moving forward, then learning as you correct, is what separates the mediocre from the great, the unprofessional from the professional.

16
BALANCING WORK AND FAMILY
Creating Your Ideal Work Schedule

"Better learn balance. Balance is key."
~ Mr. Miyagi

Hair design is a career that can often offer wonderful, sought-after flexibility. If your ideal work environment is one where you can control or negotiate your work hours—whatever the reason may be—many salons offer flexible schedules, making it a great option if you prefer to work only day times or evenings or just weekends. This can be an ideal career for hairdressers who are also students, or parents, or those who simply enjoy dedicating quality time to their personal hobbies or other business endeavors. Be aware though that if your initial goal straight out of school is to only work part-time, you will find yourself limited to certain salons and opportunities. Only you know what's right for you, and naturally your needs will change throughout the years. In the salon industry, for a full-time stylist, flexibility truly kicks into effect once you have put in the time and patience required to build a clientele. Once a solid clientele is established and you have a few years under your belt, you will have many opportunities to modify your schedule to your liking.

The salon industry has served me well in the work/life balance quest. I've been able to adjust my schedule according to my children's needs as well as my own. There are specific things you need to inquire about before you assume the salon you work for, or are thinking of working with, will be flexible enough for your lifestyle. Some salons require their employees to work specific hours, and to be present any time the salon is open—regardless if the stylist is booked or not, new to the business or a seasoned veteran of the industry. This commonly occurs in commission or salary based salons, and when you are transitioning from being an assistant to a full-time stylist. If you are on salary your employer will often require you to be there full-time to take any walk-ins or last-minute phone bookings as needed. This is understandable given the amount of time and money you both have invested. Being new on the floor has its growing pains and requirements. Being available on demand is one of them. Therefore, there is limited flexibility given to you at this time and in this scenario. If you only intend on being a stylist part-time, to help pay the bills through school or to supplement another income, chances are you are not going to work at a salon that requires you assist and be present full-time. Your income and clientele will be greatly affected by this of course, and many who believe they can begin in this business part-time get frustrated by lack of income and lose patience with the business, and often leave within a year. That's a big investment to make only to set yourself up for frustration or failure. I've spoken to many career changers who believed they could go to cosmetology school and work whenever they wanted. Of course most of them either never completed school, or got frustrated by lack of income post graduation, and abandoned their dream of becoming a hairstylist. I don't want this to happen to you.

I'll share with you some of my experiences incorporating career and scheduling flexibility throughout the past twenty years.

When my first son was born I was working at a upscale salon full-time. Shortly after his birth, my partner and I decided to move to Florida so he could take an opportunity to work for his family business, and I could stay home with our son. This move ended up being temporary and after a year we moved back and I returned to my former salon full-time. This was only an option because I did not burn any bridges with my employer. They welcomed me back, and I resumed my schedule and quickly rebuilt my clientele. Four years later I had a second son, and I decided again to take a break from the salon industry and stay home with my newborn. At that time, I was also discerning if I wanted to continue being a stylist. I was tiptoeing near burnout, though I was only twenty-eight years old. Given I had begun working in a salon at age fifteen, this questioning and burnout was understandable and natural. So I worked until my second son was born and then did not return full-time to the salon for eight years. I did eventually go back to work on Saturdays at a smaller salon near our home, which I enjoyed because I missed working. Working one day a week basically gave us a little extra fun money to play with. I took advantage of our industry's myriad of salon options and flexibility, and found a salon and schedule that could work for both me and my family.

A few years later, my children were a bit older and I found myself ready to resume working full-time again. I found a salon near our home that was higher-end and carried products I liked. It was also a place where the owner and I 'clicked.' The one thing about the hair business is you can be frank and honest with your employer. I explained to him I was looking to return full-time, but wanted to do so gradually as my clientele built up again. My years of experience gave me the ability to negotiate a flexible schedule. I began working two evenings a week and on Saturdays. Slowly I added one day and two additional afternoons. It took less than a year for me to build enough clientele that I was booked full-time. This is due to the fact I worked very hard to attract and retain new clients. I initially offered free haircuts with color, gave discounts for referrals, booked enough time with each new client to ensure that I could give a thorough consult and non-rushed haircut. I suggested they pre-book their next appointment, and always gave a few cards to my clients to pass out to their friends. I also took the time to write a personal note to each client after their initial appointment. In this note I thanked them for coming in, invited them to follow our salon on Facebook, and reminded them to pre-book their next appointment (if they had not done so already).

A thought on personal correspondence--These days most mail people receive is either a bill or an advertisement. Receiving a hand-written note is something everyone appreciates and remembers. It's a detail that's easy and valuable. Details matter in all that you do professionally. If you want to let your clients know you care and appreciate their business, writing them a personal note is a gesture that's meaningful and memorable. Refer back to chapter six for an example of a hand-written note.

In 2013, three years after returning to work full-time, I opened my own independent salon suite. This was a hard decision due to the fact that I loved the salon I worked for and the people I worked with. However... there was one thing missing again... flexibility. I found myself struggling to juggle my children's needs while being limited to only working the hours the salon was open. I opened my own loft in order to have ultimate control of my schedule and optimal flexibility, and to also schedule some free time for myself—something I needed in order to keep my sanity.

With the salon suite I had the flexibility I needed. I also had online booking, which made booking my clients a breeze. I could access my schedule with my phone, make adjustments as needed, go in early for clients, and work on previously off days if I wanted to. I had complete control of my life and schedule, yet I desperately missed the completeness of working within a salon and with a team. There are pros and cons to operating your business out of a loft type salon. I'll discuss those more in the next chapter.

If you find yourself feeling frazzled or frustrated, take a look at your work/life balance situation, then strive to adjust your day-to-day schedule accordingly. It's important to take care of yourself, and to have time to dedicate to your life outside of the salon. When you're in an industry such as ours, you give an extreme amount of energy to your career because you work directly with the public every day. Your livelihood depends on your ability to meet or exceed others' expectations on a very personal level. Creating harmony within your own personal life—by allowing time for your family, hobbies, health, pleasure and community—will bring balance to this amount of energy you dedicate to your clientele each day. This work/life balance will ensure peace of mind and a positive outlook, which will enhance your ability to take care of your clients. A happy stylist has happy clients. It's that simple.

A career within the salon industry can offer an amazing amount of flexibility, particularly after you've established yourself. And, if you decide to take extended time off for any reason, you can always return. I've focused predominately on how I've adjusted my career to suit my growing, ever-evolving family, but this same premise can be applied to any personal need. It's an industry where opportunities for flexible scheduling are plentiful. Whether you need time for your children, or yourself; for new adventures or just a time-out... there are always options to explore if you find your work/life balance out of sync.

17
INTERVIEW: ANDREA JAGELLO
Stylist of Eight (Ok, Fine... Six) Years

*"The secret of getting ahead, is getting
started." ~ Mark Twain*

I'm lucky to call Andrea Jagello my friend. We met in 2010,
when I began working at the salon she still currently works
her magic in. What I find most inspiring about Andrea is her
attention to detail. She is an absolute perfectionist who
triple checks every formula, considers every snip she's
about to take, and you can usually spot her following her
client's hair with her gaze as they're walking out the door...
always looking at her work from every angle, always making
sure it's exactly how she and her client envisioned. She is
meticulous. This attention to detail built her a loyal
following, fast. As an added bonus, she's one of the most

sincere and honest people I've ever known. I sat down with Andrea one afternoon to ask her a few questions about the business. Her newborn and my four-month-old joined us, making the interview go a lot like the days in a salon typically go—fast paced, unpredictable, and loud.

So, Andrea... how long have you been a stylist?

Almost eight years.

Really!? I had no idea you've been doing hair for that long.

Well, I was in school for part of that but I count my years in school though. When I was first beginning my career and people would ask me how long I'd been doing hair (a friend) told me to count my time in school, so I do.

Good advice. That certalnly counts. What made you want to be a hairstylist?

I just really like beauty and fashion and I like people. It's fun to make people feel pretty.

Did you work in a salon before you went to school?

Yes. And that definitely inspired me to be a hairdresser.

How many salons did you look at before choosing the salon you apprenticed with? And what made you choose the salon you decided to work for?

I looked at three different salons, and I chose the one I apprenticed in (that I'm still in now) because I liked the atmosphere and the people that worked there, and I felt like there was a lot of freedom there. It wasn't so corporate, and it seemed a lot more flexible than the other salons I looked at.

Speaking of flexibility, you just recently had a baby… how have you found the work / life balance and flexibility going now that you're a mother?

It's good. I look forward to going to work—it's nice that I have good clients that I look forward to seeing. I like my job, which makes going back to work after having a baby easier I think. The salon I work for has been very flexible with me, which is important to me. I'm sure other salons out there wouldn't quite be so flexible, ya' know. It's hard being away some days, but it's going really well.

How long did it take for you to build your clientele to the point where you felt confident in your career and ability to support yourself financially?

I would say I started feeling confident three years out of school. And as far as supporting myself, I was paid minimum wage when I went on the floor after apprenticing, and began receiving commission once my weekly totals were higher than that minimum wage, which is nothing to live on. So, I lived with my sister rent-free, and I had a second job that I went to on my off days from the salon. I began to feel confident that I could support myself about four years out of school. My apprenticeship was almost two years long, and it took me another two years after that to begin feeling secure financially.

Now I feel good, six years out of school. I'm able to go back part-time after having the baby, and I know that I'll be booked solid during those hours. But those first years are not easy.

What has surprised you most about being a hairdresser?

Being so invested in your clients—caring about them so much, considering them friends, and I would hope vice-versa.

What advice would you give someone who is just beginning their career as a stylist?

To apprentice at a salon that they want to continue to work in. I think it's really important to find a salon that you feel is a good fit.

18
THE EVOLUTION OF YOUR CAREER
Employment Options in the Salon Industry

"Pleasure in the job puts perfection in
the work." ~ Aristotle

There are several employment options in the salon industry,
and their differences are important to study and consider
when deciding what's best for you. As your career evolves,
you will naturally want to re-examine the choices you've
made and make sure the salon you're in is still in tune with
your goals and overall happiness. The salon you may have
chosen to apprentice in or begin your career in may or may
not suit you as your career advances. At one time or
another you will need to take a look at other options and
move your business if necessary. Of course, if you've signed
a contract the decision to make a move will have other

variables. Refer back to chapter four on contracts for more information on how to make this decision when legal implications are just as much a factor as personal and professional ones.

Some stylists who initially go into an hourly pay scenario realize they could make more—significantly more—if they worked elsewhere. The reasons for choosing an hourly salon are notable, and again this will depend on your needs and goals and the balance between known benefits and taking a risk. Hourly pay often provides a sense of stability that other salon work structures cannot. For example, you know exactly what you will be getting paid each week. You may also have the chance to increase this pay by receiving retail commission, bonuses and a continuous pay raise as your clientele grows. A salon with hourly pay usually (but not always) offers benefits such as health insurance, maternity or paternity leave, investment opportunities such as a 401k, as well as paid vacations and sick days. Education and products are provided for, as well as advertising and other customer incentives. Despite these benefits, it is also potentially very limiting, and I would caution against signing on for an hourly pay, especially one that does not have a clear roadmap towards pay raises or compensation, or which does not encourage maximum personal and professional growth.

Commission based salons are the most common route for both new and established stylists, but often do not offer the same benefits as hourly salons do. New stylists at commission salons receive a very small hourly pay (think minimum wage) until their weekly totals meet the criteria for going on commission (which is typically but not always double your hourly pay). It's Federal law that stylists be paid at least minimum wage for their time at the salon, and in exchange you are expected to help out during your down time (sweep hair, fold towels, help other stylists, tidy the salon as necessary—similar to the expectations of an apprentice). Once you've hit commission consistently, it's rare to slip back into hourly pay, which is great! You've hit a milestone. Your book is growing, you're too busy to clean, and you're making solid money. Note that if knowing exactly what your paycheck will be is of most importance for you, be prepared for your paycheck to fluctuate at a commission salon and plan your budget accordingly. Your pay will vary week to week, depending on your service totals. Also note that commission rates vary throughout the states, and often depend on the cost of living in that area. Ideally commission is on a sliding scale, giving you the opportunity to keep more of your income as your business grows, but that's not always the case.

For example, let's say you sign on to work at a salon with a sliding commission scale, starting at 40% commission until you reach three thousand dollars in total service sales for the pay period. After that your commission rises to 45%. Once you hit four thousand dollars in total sales, your commission increases to 50%,and so on and so on, usually capping at 60% of your totals, whether you bring in six-thousand dollars a week or ten. Very few commission salons offer more than 60% commission regardless. Most cap out at 50% commission pay, which is an ideal and generous percentage. Again, this will depend on the overhead of the salon, and benefits or incentives they pay, education expenses, etc... If you find a salon that does go higher than 50%, and you're happy working there, consider yourself very lucky. Salons with sliding commission scales have loads of benefits in that you essentially go to work, do your job, have opportunity for growth, sometimes but not always have all or partial health insurance coverage, and you typically do not need to pay for the products or color you use on clients. You may also receive education provided by the salon, as well as a paid vacation. In regards to commission based salons, I would recommend you seek out salons with a sliding commission scale for when you're established. Sliding commission scales coupled with appropriate, well-thought-out price increases, work together towards a path of financial success and professional growth and compensation.

Booth rental is an option for more established stylists who consistently bring in a stable income and would like to pay a flat rental rate to their salon owner (i.e. landlord) instead of a commission based on their totals. In booth rental, there are no benefits such as health care, etc., but you do make on average thirty percent more than if you were on commission. That extra income should be applied towards providing your own insurance and retirement plans, but no one is going to tell you what to do with your money. There's also more freedom, because as a booth renter you create your own work schedule and prices. Some salons give their booth renters a key so they can come and go and work as they please. Other salons do require booth renters work within established pre-determined salon hours. Booth renters must pay for all their products and color, as well as pay for their continuing education, marketing and advertising, and are solely responsible for maintaining and growing their clientele. They also are typically responsible for booking and confirming their clients' appointments. Since a majority of solid client growth is obtained through word-of-mouth, the art of keeping your clientele growing and flowing and a solid knowledge of the business side of running a salon should be firmly established before venturing into a booth rental situation. Also, your average weekly income needs to be thoroughly scrutinized before you decide to go on your own.

Here's an example of when booth rental would work, and when it would not:

Let's say your average weekly sales totals are $2500.00. At a 50% commission rate, your adjusted sales total would be $1250.00. Let's estimate thirty percent of your gross paycheck is taken out for taxes. This would leave you with a weekly net paycheck of $875.00. (Divide this by 40, and that's approx $21.00 per hour.)

Now let's say you go to a booth rental salon and again, your average weekly sales totals are $2500. And let's say your booth rental fee for the week is $250.00. This leaves you with $2250.00 as your weekly gross income after rent. You still need to take out your taxes, so again at a 30% tax rate your adjusted net income is now $1575.00. (Divide this by a 40 hour work week, and you're making $39.00 per hour.) That's $700.00 more than if you were to remain on commission. However, keep in mind in booth rental you must provide your own products—from shampoo to styling products, color, everything…. as well as any insurance (healthcare, disability, etc.) education, and retirement savings options. If you opt for online booking and other customer service programs, that cost is covered by you as well. These necessary expenses add up, so be prepared and do your math carefully before you go out on your own and booth rent.

Booth rental would not work if your numbers are erratic, and are so low that after paying rent, taxes, and product costs you're left with little to no income increase. Sure you may have freedom, but so do unemployed people technically. You just don't have any money.

Stylists and salon owners have vastly different opinions towards booth rental salons. They are a divisive topic. Some say they provide an ideal work environment in regards to freedom, flexibility and opportunity for established hair designers. Others loathe the idea of a non-cohesive team where every man works and looks out for himself, and the greater good of the salon and team is non-existent. In a booth rental situation, salon owners are basically landlords who have no say in their stylists' day-to-day work, which dilutes any chance of having a salon image or team that works together. Some believe the extra administrative work that comes along with being a booth renter makes the scenario not worth it financially. Others wouldn't have it any other way. It all comes down to you, your goals, your business know-how, and what 'feels' right.

Another (and equally divisive) option in our industry is the independent salon suite, sometimes called 'loft salons,' 'boutique salons,' 'concept salons,' 'studio salons' etc... Love 'em or loathe them, they are emerging as an interesting and lucrative option for those who wish to rent their own space outside the confines of a 'traditional' salon. Trends show significant projected growth for suite-style salons throughout the country. In a loft-style salon, you have the freedom to work whatever hours you wish—allowing you to schedule appointments during times that work best for you and your clients. You can decorate how you wish, carry whatever products you desire, and run your business as you see fit. No one else is involved in your decision making. It can be very worthwhile and rewarding. Keep in mind you are running a business. Similar to booth rental, you and you alone are responsible for keeping track of your income and reporting all your earnings to the IRS for tax purposes. You also have to keep a close eye on your color inventory and product inventory—you, and only you, are responsible for every aspect of running an efficient salon. Running out of color, products, towels, etc., is not an option. You're also responsible for marketing yourself and attracting new clients. You have to wash all your towels and keep your studio clean. A loft salon has its pros and cons, and for many the pros outweigh the cons, and in time you will get into a routine that is anything but a burden. I had a loft before my third child was born and learned a lot from the experience. Would I do it again? Probably not. However, many of my friends run lofts and thoroughly enjoy it.

I've worked hourly, on commission, and have operated my own salon suite. My advice is that you not let fear deter you when making career decisions. If hourly works best for you, do it. If commission's where you're most comfortable, there are many privately owned salons that need you and want your talent desperately. And if you've reached a point in your career where running your own show meets your needs best, and booth rental or a studio environment appeals to you, go for it. The goal is to continue growing as a stylist and more importantly, as a human being. Every person's scenario and needs are different, and only you know what's best for you both financially and personally.

I will share my perspective and experience over the years, and why I chose to open my own loft, because there are a few components to working out of a loft that I failed to ponder fully, that I feel are important to share with you. As suite style salons continue to grow in popularity, I feel it's important to cover this option in more detail and on a personal level. For one, you lose the team aspect of working in a salon—one that exists whether you're on commission or sometimes in booth rental. You no longer have a co-worker beside you to bounce ideas off of or chat with during down time or while working. Co-workers can inspire and help when needed, something to never take for granted. Lofts are often so small there's no room for error in timing your services, and in a pinch there's no one there to lend a helping hand, or seek advice from when you're unsure of the best way to go about a process.

I can only recommend booth rental or a loft-style salon to those who are well established and experienced, and who are comfortable working independently. I personally found I truly missed my co-workers. Now, I was lucky enough to work in a small salon with fantastic people before moving to the loft. I was very happy with my work environment. If you'd prefer to work independently then a salon suite might be the ideal situation for you. I moved into an independent salon solely for the benefit of making my own schedule and working around the needs of my growing family. Because I was limited to the hours of the commission salon I was working in, and I couldn't access my schedule online or rearrange it as needed, I had hit a wall both professionally and personally. I wanted to work around my son's school schedule, plus work additional hours that were unavailable to me in the traditional salon setting. It was a tough decision, but one I do not regret, based solely on all that I learned.

When you're at a career crossroads, remember to look at all the options. Before I went to a loft space I looked for over a year. There were lofts available sooner, but they were too small and felt closed in. And loft spaces, in general, are small. But there are benefits to their size as well. Many clients feel like they are in their own personal hair salon. They feel comfortable enough to speak freely; they don't feel funny about sitting around with wet hair or color on their hair within a room full of people. The more intimate feel allows them to communicate even more authentically. And during the times I was double booked at the loft, often the two clients within my space found a connection with each other, forged new friendships, and it was rarely awkward. If I sensed ahead of time two people might not get along, or that a client would prefer to be the only client in my space for his or her services, I booked their appointments accordingly. Remember, above all, people want to relax during their services and leave feeling good. They want intimacy and comfort. A loft can provide this atmosphere beautifully. Just be aware of these needs when decorating your space and booking your clients. You cannot cram a haircut in. You cannot run behind. You cannot run out of color or ask a co-worker for help or advice. What you can do is give the ultimate personal experience. You can make your space reflect your personality. You can make your own hours and accommodate clients with special needs.

Loft style salons typically include online booking services with no additional cost to the stylist. Others require you to book your clients the old-fashioned way via the phone. If you choose the phone booking option (or if that's the only way available to you) keep in mind you will be on your phone a lot. I recommend having a separate business phone line. Online booking is the best option, for both the stylist and the client. I found my clients absolutely loved being able to schedule their appointments online. In fact, they loved it so much, I would advise all salons to offer this option.

The evolution of a stylist's career often finds many stylists working at some point in all of these scenarios. You may begin somewhere hourly, work up or move to commission, eventually run your own salon or loft or booth rent... in the salon industry you are not limited to one particular business model. This is another rare gift being a hairdresser gives. We have options, and as long as you are happy and your clients are happy, you can succeed anywhere that suits you best.

19
EXIT STRATEGY
Moving From One Salon to the Next

"If you do not feel yourself growing in your work and your life broadening and deepening, if your task is not a perpetual tonic to you, you have not found your place."
~ Orison Swett Marden

Very few stylists, if any, stay with the same salon or company their entire career. There are an infinite amount of reasons why stylists seek a new work space. These reasons can be practical or personal. Regardless, it's important to leave a salon with as much professional grace as you can muster. It's an unfortunate reality of our business that often when you choose to leave one salon for another, it can get ugly.

It's important to be as honest as possible when telling a salon owner you no longer wish to work with them. However, honest does not mean harsh. The salon industry is a tight one. Sometimes you cannot avoid burning bridges but it is important to go in with the intent of remaining respectful of each other after your parting. Salon owners often understand, and some are relieved, when you leave. That does not mean they aren't also going to panic at the thought of you taking business away from them. I do advise giving them notice—two weeks is standard in nearly every industry. But be prepared for many salons to tell you to leave right away. Some salon owners allow and encourage you to stay, but for the most part they do not want you to have the opportunity to tell your clients of your plans while operating in their space. The sooner you leave, the less opportunity you have to inform and take your clientele with you.

That being said, make sure before you tell your current employer of your plans that you are prepared to walk out the door immediately—have all your 'ducks in a row' so to speak. Some people schedule a little vacation time for the transition; others begin at their new salon space the very next day. Just be prepared. Very rarely will a salon owner, once informed a stylist is leaving, allow a stylist to stay another day.

When I left the salon I was working at to open my loft salon, I was allowed to stay during the transition. However, I did agree to not speak to my clientele openly about my move while in the salon, and I honored that agreement. This is a highly unusual scenario. I'll share with you the reasons why it worked out so gracefully.

First of all, I wasn't leaving because I was unhappy or bitter or treated poorly. There was no tension or bad blood between my employer and me. I had simply hit a point in my career where it was necessary for me to control my time completely. I tend to look ahead and plan accordingly, and after re-evaluating my current life work/life balance goals, I decided it was most important for me to slow down a bit. I had hit a level of exhaustion that I felt was keeping me from doing anything properly—pulled in so many directions I collapsed most nights on the couch with my shoes still on. I decided to explore an independent loft salon. I knew if I opened my own loft, I could arrange my schedule to fit my personal life and growing family. I also knew after my initial investment I'd make about the same amount of money part-time as I did full-time in my current commission situation. And as much as I loved my co-workers, I knew the salon owner would not be able to accommodate my needs and remain fair to the other employees. I needed full flexibility, online booking, and more money—three things he could not provide for me.

So, I told the salon owner and manager exactly what I just shared with you. I had to make changes in order to bring balance to my life. I told them of my plans before my loft was ready—taking a huge risk, because financially I needed to work seamlessly. I also told them my plans without having any knowledge of what my book looked like for the next few months. I knew most of my clients pre-booked, but I did not have access to that book nor any ethical way of gathering that very important information. I did the unthinkable. I asked them for my future schedule. I also asked them for my client list.

They did the unthinkable—they gave me both.

How did this go so well? I was honest and completely transparent with them. I didn't try anything shady out of fear. I showed them respect, and in return they showed me respect as well. I was able to transfer my booked clients onto my new schedule. I had every client's phone number and address as well.

If you're a commissioned or hourly salon employee, there are some ethical and legal issues to consider when leaving a salon. First of all, it is illegal to get into the salon computer system and steal your client list. I know you feel they are your clients, and I often will agree—a majority of them come to the salon to see you, not for the salon décor. However, if you try to obtain client information by removing it from the salon database without the salon's consent, that is considered illegal and the salon could, if they so chose, prosecute. Booth renters do not run into this scenario because they keep their own client information. (Some commission salons will allow you to keep your own records, but most will not.)

Fortunately, modern technology has alleviated some of the

stress and worry over how to stay in contact with your clientele. Social media sites such as Facebook are not only great marketing tools, but also legal ways to inform your clientele of your business happenings. (As discussed in chapter 14, I highly recommend using social media as an avenue for staying connected with your clientele.)

I understand my experience leaving a prior salon is a rare one. Having worked in a salon for the better part of twenty years, I've watched stylists depart under terrible circumstances. When I worked the front desk I had to field calls from clients wondering where their stylist was, and I was told specifically to not give any information to clients. When a stylist quits—or worse, when there's a walkout (several stylists leaving at once)—it's an uncomfortable and stressful situation for everyone involved.

There's always the risk of losing clientele when you switch salons. Most will follow you, and some will not. Here is a testimonial from a client as to why she left a stylist due to a salon change:

"Typically I look for a combination of elements to come together to provide a great haircut and salon experience. Over many years I followed one stylist from place to place— five different salons in total. During this time it was the confidence I had knowing I was going to get a great haircut coupled with the great salon vibe. I enjoyed the different salon atmospheres and architecture. I decided to leave my stylist though when he moved to a loft salon. It was way too boxy (claustrophobic) and small and I felt like I was getting

my hair done in a closet."

This is an interesting testimonial, because the client followed her stylist to five different locations over the years. She clearly was devoted. However, it wasn't something the stylist did to her hair that made her leave. It was his choice of salons that finally made her switch. He chose to open his own space within a concept/loft-style salon—something that's emerging as one of the strongest options for an independent stylist, and something I've done as well. Her feelings were that the salon space felt too small and boxy.

It's unfortunate this stylist lost his client due to his new salon environment. But that's bound to happen. Obviously he's very talented—she followed him to five other salons. Always remember, not every single client is going to follow you when you move. But if the move is in your best interest, and benefits the majority of your clientele as well, then it's worth it. Many stylists are afraid to move because they worry their clients won't follow them. Remember you can't please everyone all the time. The handful of clients that may not follow you have their own reasons for doing so— perhaps your new choice is too far away, they don't like the new space you're going to, or they were contemplating a new stylist anyway. Maybe, like the testimonial above, they are sensitive to salon size and atmosphere. You should be aware of the majority of your clients' needs and expectations while staying focused on the big picture— which is, where are you going to thrive? The big picture has you in the middle, with many components and considerations branching out from there. Remember, a happy stylist has happy clients. And happiness is contagious.

Previously I recommended sending your new clients hand-written thank-you notes—thanking them for giving you the opportunity to be their hairstylist—after their initial visit with you. I also highly recommended you notify your clients of your new salon in the same fashion. This task may seem daunting, and it will take time to complete, but again nothing is more personal than a hand-written letter. It is acceptable to draw up a form letter (that you still personally sign) in this instance. In this letter you should state the obvious—the new salon you'll be working at, how much you've appreciated their business over the years, and that you're looking forward to sharing this experience with them, etc. Remember to include your new business card, and although it's not necessary, offering a discount on their first appointment with you at your new space is a nice way to show you appreciate their support. Here's one example of how your letter could look:

Dear Beyoncé,

I'm excited to inform you that as of Jan 1st, 2015, I will be moving my business to The Best Hair Salon Ever, located at 1234 Main Street. I'm looking forward to sharing this adventure with you, and can't wait to see you at my new space. I truly appreciate your loyalty over the years, so as a thank-you, I'm offering ten percent off your next service with me at The Best Hair Salon Ever. Call 555-5555 to schedule your next appointment. I look forward to seeing you soon!

Sincerely,
Your Ever-Evolving Awesome Hairstylist

P.S. If you haven't done so already, stay connected with me via Facebook (insert Facebook page name) or Twitter (insert Twitter information.) All of the new salon information is available there as well. If you have any questions, feel free to call or message me!

If your new salon offers services your previous salon did not (such as spa services, online booking, etc.) it's nice to mention the new services now available to your clientele in your letter as well. The key is to keep it positive and brief— show your personality, enthusiasm towards your new venture, and appreciation for your clientele.

Leaving one salon for another (whether it's a new space, opening your own salon or salon suite, or what have you...) can be stressful but it is often very exciting. Let that excitement carry you forward.

20
BURNOUT
Warning Signs, and How to Deal With It

"There is virtue in work and there is virtue in rest. Use both and overlook neither."
~ Alan Cohen

One fact about working in the salon industry is when you're at work, you have to be 'on' constantly. There's no room for your bad mood, disappointing evening, or frazzled morning commute to surface when you're working one-on-one with a client. You have to love to talk, and more importantly, listen; be engaged all day, every day, for hours and hours on end.

Some will say this is the best part of their day. Others will say it drains them completely. It's a myth that all hairstylists are extroverts. In fact, many are quiet introverted creatives and we need them to bring balance to the work space. Regardless if you're quiet or boisterous, our job is quite often draining—physically, mentally and emotionally—and at the end of the day we just want to put our feet up and zone out in front of the TV.

What this can create is little to no work/life balance. You may find you give 100% at work, leaving you with little or no energy for anything else. You may find you have a million friends in the way of clients at work, and absolutely no social life or friends outside of the salon.

This, my friends, is the path to Hairdresser Burnout.

Merriam-Webster defines burnout as "the condition of someone who has become very physically and emotionally tired after doing a difficult job for a long time."

There's no escaping feeling burnout in this industry. Usually, it just means you need a vacation and a re-evaluation of your work/life balance. Sometimes, it's a sign you need to re-evaluate your career goals. And sometimes, if left unaddressed, it means it's time to put the shears away for awhile.

Burnout is near impossible to hide in the salon. Even if you haven't acknowledged, addressed, or admitted to your feelings, they show through your client relations, your interactions with co-workers, and the quality of your work. You may find you don't want to talk to your clients or co-workers as much, perhaps even waking up with a sense of dread about your day. Instead of a full book making you feel happy and secure, it irritates you and makes you feel like you never get a break. You may begin making mistakes— not quite finishing a haircut as detailed as you normally would, or missing spots in a color application and not really caring enough to correct either. You call in sick when you're not, or feel sick even though nothing is wrong with you. Basically, you feel disengaged. If any of this sounds familiar, you most likely are burnt out and need a break.

Don't feel bad about taking a break. In fact, it's very important that you do. We give so much of ourselves daily to our clients it can be exhausting and overwhelming. Our job is both emotionally draining and physically demanding. The trick is to schedule time off, have a vacation or down-time planned ahead so you can regularly step back and take time just for you. Often once burnout creeps in, we begin beating ourselves up over it—asking the big questions like, "what am I supposed to be doing with my life, am I in the right career, what is the point" and so on and so on. While these philosophical questions certainly deserve attention, before you hop into a tornado of career despair, take a step back and get some rest. If you can't afford a vacation, find an outside hobby and or mind-body practice you enjoy, so your energy resources have a chance to be refilled. I personally couldn't function at work if I didn't have the balance yoga and creative writing bring to my life. The happiest stylists I know have interests outside of work that fulfill them and offset the extreme amount of energy we give to others each day.

Take a look at your work/life balance goals and adjust accordingly. If the existential questions persist, there's no harm or shame in seeing a therapist. Sometimes, the simplest change brings about the greatest result. A daily walk and paying attention to your diet could be just the change you need. Education, giving yourself proper pay raises, and challenging yourself are all key to avoiding burnout as well. If you're not continuously inspired, challenged and compensated for your hard work, most likely you will grow bitter and depressed.

Tips to Avoid Burnout:

Have a vacation planned at least twice a year. Figure out your budget, put money aside, and then take some time for you. Downtime, whether it's a simple three day weekend at home, or an extravagant vacation, is not a luxury it's a necessity.

Invest in your well being. Find a hobby, physical activity or interest group to join (writing, design, gardening, culinary… whatever!) and make taking care of you a priority. Yoga and massage therapy are excellent ways to decompress, and both also help repair our bodies from the physical demands of our industry.

Know when to say "no." Clients will ask for favors, such as "squeezing them in" or coming in on an off day. Some may ask you to do their hair at home. Some may ask for a special rate or a freebie. Your friends and family will ask all of these things from you. Learn when to say "no," and don't feel the least bit bad about it. You need and deserve time off too. Set boundaries, and keep them.

We take care of people all day long. It can be incredibly draining. To avoid burnout, take time to take care of you.

21
SWITCHING GEARS
Becoming a Hairstylist As a Second Career

"Whatever you can do or dream you can do, begin it. Boldness has genius, power and magic in it." ~Goethe

We all have dreams, and then make choices that either bring us closer to our dreams or push us father away. Some of us know exactly what we want to be when we grow up. Many of us don't know until we are a bit older and can visualize a clearer picture. Often it takes years of experiencing what we don't want in order to go after what we do. Deciding to go back to school later in life to pursue a second career can be daunting and scary. If being a hairstylist is what you truly desire, and what you see yourself doing, know that many people do go to cosmetology school later in life and go on to have very successful careers in the salon industry. Do not let your age or uncertainty deter you. In fact, your age will work to your benefit. You most likely will pay closer attention, make solid career decisions, and gain respect from your clients and peers due to the prior world and business experience you've accumulated outside of the salon industry.

The first step is finding the right cosmetology school, and that will depend greatly on your day-to-day schedule and whether or not you plan to go to school full-time or part-time. Flexibility and cost are two of the most important factors when you're an adult choosing to go back to school. My advice is to tour every school in your area before making a choice. And, if you can, spend an entire day there.

I'm going to share three very different stories with you—friends and colleagues who have pursued hairstyling as second career paths. I'll begin with an amazing woman in her forties who went to school with me when I was nineteen. She was an artist, a visual and tactile learner, who always wanted to be a hairdresser. Mid-way through school she dropped out because she was not emotionally prepared to be surrounded by people in their late teens and early twenties. She panicked. She was someone I respected, and we had a good friendship while she was in school. I admired her for returning to school. She gave me a card and a gift she designed when she left school. I still have her card and gift box today—twenty years later. I was sad and disappointed she quit, but I understood why. She felt she had embarked on the wrong path. Perhaps she hadn't visited enough schools before signing up to see who her peers would be, and therefore hadn't given herself time to digest and accept her new, though temporary, reality. She was shy, creative, and emanated quiet dignity—I believe she would have made a good hairstylist, with a kind clientele.

Another acquaintance shared with me her story of going to cosmetology school later in life. I share her story because it is one I've seen and heard many times over and I don't want it to happen to you should you make this decision. She went to cosmetology school full-time, graduated, and landed a job at small, established salon near her home. She was divorced, had two children, and obviously needed steady income. She soon discovered how difficult it was to build a clientele your first year out of school and within six months had quit and gone back to her old job. There were several factors leading to this scenario, one of them being the salon she chose was not one that advertised or promoted itself in any way. She also was unprepared—unaware of how much time and effort it can take to build a client base inside a salon that does not attract new clients regularly. Choosing another salon and doing her research would have made her first year and therefore her long term career as a stylist more viable. She needed a salon that recognized and supported her. That is why regardless if you're eighteen or forty, interviewing several salons and outlining your requirements and needs is a must. Do not risk setting yourself up for failure by not exploring all your options and finding a salon that supports you and your career.

Now I share with you the success story of a man who left his lucrative corporate job to become a hairstylist. I had the pleasure of working with him for many years, and respect his work ethic immensely. Because he was in the business world for so long he brought with him a level of professionalism and dedication that I believe led to his success. Of course you don't need a corporate background to become a successful hairstylist. It all comes down to drive, work ethic, belief in and respect for yourself, professionalism, and determination. I asked him to share some advice with those who are debating pursuing hairstyling as a second career. Here's what he had to say:

"Conduct informational interviews with experienced stylists. Consider shadowing multiple stylists at different salons. Select the best school you can afford. Interview them and spend a day there. When selecting a salon to work in, interview with a wide variety of salons. Choose a salon that has plenty of walk-ins. Never sign a non-compete agreement. Consider working part-time at a salon as a receptionist while attending school. Make sure you have a passion for hair and enjoy being in the service industry. Be patient!"

He successfully embarked on his new career as a stylist because he knew the right questions to ask, made thoughtful decisions, stayed patient, and ultimately chose the right salon to work with. The salon was successful, advertised, had a busy staff and new clients calling in daily, and required an apprenticeship before letting you on the floor. He was tipped out properly each day by his mentor and clients, and paid a base salary until he consistently hit his weekly goal for commission. The salon offered health insurance and a 401k. He did his research and chose the right salon for his needs. His success wasn't luck—it was the result of having a goal, pursuing a dream, and a well-crafted plan.

This industry is fueled by passion and determination. If you've always wanted to be a hairdresser, you should be. Do not be afraid to go back to school. Go in with your head held high. Your age is a blessing. Remember to research and interview several schools and salons before committing. There is a salon out there waiting for someone dedicated and daring like you; a mentor ready to take you under their wing and make this the best career decision you've ever made.

22
WHY HAIR?
Because You're Awesome, That's Why

"Too bad all the people who know how to run the country are busy driving taxi cabs and cutting hair." ~ George Burns

Somewhere along the road people are going to ask you why you wanted to, or want to be, a hairstylist. Every single one of us will have a unique answer, but there's a commonality between stylists that also makes us unified in our answer to the question, "Why Hair?"

My answer to this question has evolved over time, as I suspect it will for you too. In the beginning I would tell those who asked that I loved playing with hair; that as a child my little sisters, cousins and friends were my first clients, whether they wanted to be or not—and that later, when I got my first job as a receptionist in a hair salon, I would watch the stylists and be amazed by their creativity and lack of fear. I couldn't believe they could hold a conversation with ease while cutting someone's hair. They made it look so effortless and fun. And it was fun. I absorbed and observed so much while working the front desk. I was inspired and knew it was what I had to do.

Twenty years later I'd say it all comes down to the human connection. I yearn for and have come to need the relationships, the bonding, the giving and the receiving, between humans that being a hairstylist brings. Perhaps it was this connection I was seeking all along.

Just as each and every client is unique, so is every stylist. At our core, those of us called to this profession share many traits. We intuitively need to work with our hands. We are visual thinkers. We see things in color, shapes, lines, and textures. We are artistic. We are creative and sensitive. We are people pleasers, whether we want to admit that or not. We like to talk. We need to express ourselves. We take pleasure in a job well done, in results we can immediately see. Though we have many creative talents, hair is the vessel we chose and use to connect with the people and world around us.

Every day I see anywhere from four to fifteen people in my chair—each client bringing their own energy into the space, merging it with mine. I love that. I love working so intimately with them. I love having conversations and hearing fresh perspectives I wouldn't have been exposed to otherwise. I love the laughter that often echoes throughout a hair salon. It goes so far beyond the hair cut or color. It's so much more. People go to the hairstylist when they're happy, when they're sad, when they need a self-esteem boost and when they want to present themselves confidently to the world. They mark special times in their lives, as well as periods of change, with a new haircut or style. They save their babies' first snips, and lovingly style their grandmother's hair. Hairstylists are an important part in the lives of their clientele, playing a vital role behind the scenes of many beautiful memories and milestones.

Nostalgia and sentiment aside, people spend a significant amount of time and money on their appearance and grooming. Consider that job security. Hair is big business. Being a hairstylist can not only provide satisfying financial rewards, but it's one of the few professions that absolutely cannot be replaced by a computer, a machine, or be outsourced for greater profit. When recessions hit our economy, we feel a slight pinch, but nothing compared to other industries. From my experience, clients will cut back on many areas before they skimp on their hair. And during economic downturns, those who are job seeking certainly do not hold back on their personal grooming. They know looking good for an interview is half the battle. Growth will continue throughout this industry, for as populations grow there will be an even greater need for hairstylists in the future. That means more employment options for stylists, and greater opportunity to make the most out of your chosen profession.

Perhaps you are drawn to hairstyling because you are drawn to people. Perhaps you simply enjoy playing with hair, or are obsessed with style, color, shapes and textures. Maybe you're seeking a secure artistic profession with financial stability. Maybe you just want a career that is fun yet challenging.

Whatever the reason, the good news is, in this industry you can have all of this and more.

In your hands you have a guide to understanding the beauty industry and making the most out of your career. I wish you immense success and would love to hear your story.

Contact: BusinessofBeautyBook@gmail.com
Follow: @BizBeautyBook on Twitter
Connect: Carrie Herzner via LinkedIn
Like: Business of Beauty Book on Facebook
Visit: www.businessofbeautybook.com

ABOUT THE AUTHOR

Carrie Herzner has spent over twenty years in the salon industry. Having worked in nearly every facet of the business, she has a deep understanding of what it takes to be a successful, professional, and happy hairstylist. She is also a published creative writer, focusing on non-fiction, memoir and personal essay. The Business of Beauty unites her passion for the salon industry with her ability to put real life experiences into context, benefiting others looking to thrive in this deeply rewarding and unique career.

Made in the USA
Middletown, DE
16 July 2015